ON BECOMING BREAD

I welcome the publication of Mary Marrocco's reflections in On Becoming Bread. Here is a person whose mind and heart probe the connections between a parent's request for a child's baptism and need for diapers, links the meeting of saintly monks in the desert with the Week of Prayer for Christian Unity, and describes the Ecumenical Patriarch's passion for ecology. These short essays inform, puzzle, surprise, and delight—sometimes all at once. They will help disciples of the Lord Jesus make the connections between their experiences and their lives as believers.

+TERRENCE PRENDERGAST, SJ,
Archbishop of Ottawa

Mary Marrocco takes the truths of Scripture and tradition and the insights of the academy of theology and runs them through the kitchens, malls, hospitals, social circles, and church circles within which she moves, and then, as best her imagination can give expression to, she gives us theology and spirituality. Sometimes she does this too in reverse, with the same effect: She takes a poignant moment from an encounter she has had and runs it through the prism of academic theology and church tradition to see what kind of a theological expression a given moment of life might take. This book is theology and spirituality as they should be done.

RONALD ROLHEISER,
President of the Oblate School of Theology,
San Antonio, Texas

on becoming bread

bread

REFLECTIONS *and* STORIES
to NOURISH YOUR SPIRIT

Dr. Mary Marrocco

TWENTY-THIRD
PUBLICATIONS
twentythirdpublications.com

DEDICATED TO

MY FATHER AND MOTHER,

DOMINIC MARROCCO

& RITA LARSEN

Twenty-Third Publications
One Montauk Avenue, Suite 200
New London, CT 06320
(860) 437-3012 or (800) 321-0411
www.twentythirdpublications.com

Cover photo: iStockphoto.com / aprilante

ISBN: 978-1-62785-444-3
Library of Congress Control Number: 2018962308
Printed in the U.S.A.

 A division of Bayard, Inc.

TABLE OF CONTENTS

PROLOGUE

It was a lively day at St. John the Compassionate Mission: lunch for a hundred was being prepared by volunteers, the drop-in was swirling with comers and goers, crises little and large waxed and waned. The usual. In those days, I was assisting at this inner-city mission, which invited neighborhood folks to share meals, work, prayer, and time together as they needed. The mission housed a parish, also available to the neighborhood.

While working at the Mission, I was engaged in my doctorate in theology at a Catholic institution, reading and studying some of the greatest teachers the church has ever known. Working there complemented my studies in ways I could never have planned but was coming to see more and more.

On this day, a young couple came to visit with their little one in his stroller. We'd known the couple, Tom and Mildred, for some time but hadn't seen them since the baby's birth. Both lived on welfare and had often dropped in for meals. Today, they'd come in to ask about having their child baptized. As they were leaving, Tom turned to me saying, "Oh, by the way, do you have any diapers? The checks won't be out till Friday and we're all out."

As I went to our storage room to find a package, the combination bemused me: baptism and diapers. Once again, "the poor" were teaching me about the church: it's concerned with baptism *and* diapers. The church's liturgy touches real life in all its mundane glory; and real life reaches into the liturgy, the sacraments, spirituality, and life of the church. It's supposed to. God became

1

human, flesh and spirit, body and soul, just as we are. When we call the church the "body" of Christ, we really mean it. Tom didn't hesitate to ask the church for diapers, any more than he hesitated to ask it for baptism. To him it seemed natural that the church should think of both. And isn't it? Can the church nourish the soul and forget the body, touch the spirit but not arouse the mind, answer the longings of the heart without engaging in the social and practical lives of its members?

For me, Tom posed the question: What is all this theology for, if not for the daily lives of regular people? "Regular people" had helped me to pursue my higher studies. Three years earlier, I'd been working as a pastoral assistant in a parish. I saw the parish as the lifeblood of the church, and I enjoyed the engagement with parishioners from whom I learned constantly. After a couple of years there, I wanted to return to school and study beyond the Master of Divinity I already had, but was torn about leaving the parish.

On Holy Saturday, following that parish's tradition, a small coterie of parishioners was preparing the church for the Easter Vigil. Several people were going to be received into the church that evening, which meant extensive preparation of many kinds. The workers (mostly women whom I'd come to know fairly well in my time there) and I spent much of the day together. They knew I was contemplating leaving them to accept the Toronto School of Theology's invitation to the doctoral program. As we ironed, cleaned, organized, rehearsed, programmed, catechized, decorated, and otherwise set up for the service, they kindly talked over my decision with me, as though I'd been their sister. The gist of what they said to me that day was: "You can do this, and we can't, because we're doing other things. We need it as much as you do. You go get that education, then come back and teach us. Do it for all of us."

This commissioning stayed with me. I couldn't help but notice that the theologians I was studying, including St. Augustine,

ON BECOMING BREAD

on whom I wrote my dissertation, thought theology should be engaged in daily life, not set apart from it. It was Augustine who, as a young man, sided with his friend Licentius against his mother, Monica, when she chastised Licentius for singing a psalm while in the restroom. Theology and prayer are for everywhere and everything, he assured them both. Though known for the written word (and he wrote many), Augustine liked images; his theology was often earthy. Living in northern Africa, in times of great suffering, he frequently reflected that people are like olives and the world like an olive press; if the people, when pressed, become pure oil, they will be treasured in jars for Christ. Augustine loved olive oil, and he loved bread. He delighted in reflecting on Jesus who becomes bread for his people, in self-giving love and above all in Eucharist. "Behold what you are," Augustine urged in contemplating the Eucharist, "become what you receive."

What could it mean to become eucharistic bread? Surely, it means being more like Christ, and therefore closer to God. Our daily lives can become daily bread for others. Our whole lives can become a self-offering. It is not easy, but it is possible, and visible all around us. Theology is not what we talk about, but how we live.

After completing my doctorate, I brought all my learning about lived theology to a new work, that of being a psychotherapist. From it, too, I daily learn about the meaning of theology—that is, about the nature of God's relationship with us, God who "loves each one of us as though there were only one of us" (Augustine again). St. John Chrysostom saw the church as a hospital and Christ as our physician, who pitched his tent among us to bring not judgment but healing.

"Whether you turn to the right or to the left, your ears will hear a voice behind you, saying 'This is the way; walk in it'" (Isaiah 30:21). I'm grateful to have been guided by that voice through the years, and to have heard it on the lips of many teachers, such as Tom and Mildred, the women of my parish, and Augustine of

Hippo. The way I've walked has been nothing I could have found on my own.

It led me, through a mutual friend, to have coffee one day with the editor of a Catholic newspaper. He was wondering how best to speak to young and older adults about things that matter to them, adults who might be searching for faith or searching to know their faith better. I told him about my quest for lived theology, and the life and faith questions I'd been hearing from adults I worked with, who came from all kinds of faith and non-faith. The two of us looked at each other with a sense of recognition.

Thus was born "Questioning Faith" (I owe my ever-creative, next-oldest brother, Bernard, for the title), my regular column in which life questions and faith questions commingle and dance with each other. These writings generally begin with questions. Some I've heard from people I know or work with. Some I've heard posed in writings or by life itself, social concerns like abortion or poverty or euthanasia, theological concerns like sin and salvation, church concerns like intercommunion and care for the bereaved. Some are specific questions readers have asked me to address. My aim is to stand up to these questions with a moment in the church's life: a teaching, a feast day, a saint or renowned Christian, a liturgical expression, a hymn. How do these church moments engage or rephrase the question, what new questions do they raise, and where do they lead us? Do they touch the grit and spit and delight and night of what really happens to us and what we genuinely wonder over, exclaim at, love and seek?

This questioning determines my trajectory in each writing. I want to fulfill my commission—to give back to "regular people" the theology I was privileged to study—to become bread for them.

As I look back over years of writing these columns, I reflect on comments, questions, and criticisms I've heard from readers, which have greatly assisted me to grow in my work. I discover certain themes that have, unprogrammed, appeared and reappeared in them, showing up in their own time like unexpected guests and coming back again intermittently like old and dear friends. Now, in *On Becoming Bread*, I have reworked and grouped my articles together under these themes: not because I set out to address them systematically (I didn't), but because I discovered in the writing and living that they are what these writings are about.

We have a questioning faith. We question it, and it questions us. The poet Rainer Maria Rilke "learned to love the questions." They lead us into all sorts of intriguing and even holy places. These days we tend to talk about faith as though it were a supermarket item one could select or reject; some people take it and some don't, and indeed it comes in different varieties which also are a matter of taste. Faith is not like that. Faith means grasping in this earthly life, by some inner means, what our external senses, understanding, and reason catch in glimmers and hints, hiddenly but persistently: "I see now as in a mirror, darkly" (1 Corinthians 13:12). Faith is a dim but true perception of reality, beyond the unnumbered universes whose existence scientists postulate but which stagger the human comprehension. That's why it's so incredibly, urgently necessary.

Faith is not at odds with reason, or with science, or with everything that happens to us in the day-to-day. No, these things educate our faith, and our faith in turn illumines them. We need not leave it on the shelf as an extra accessory, or toss it in the trash bin as an obsolete appendage. We need it now, not in some future heaven, or after retirement when we have leisure for it and for gardening. We need to work with it, "toss it and roll it, and pat it and pat it," as my mother used to say as she taught me to make bun dough. Maybe our faith is the bun dough, or maybe we ourselves are; in any case, the tossing and rolling will raise it up and make it bake up golden and beautiful, ready for its true Maker who became bread for us and taught us to become bread for one another.

Encounter

Ever ancient, ever new

One of the three things that give meaning, according to Viktor Frankl, is an encounter with someone or something. An encounter I once had made me seek the meaning of trust.

I hadn't seen my friend Ed in a couple of years; he'd gone one direction to attend school, and I'd gone another for a new job. Now he was in the hospital, critically ill.

Seeing Ed's name beside the door I'd been directed to, I entered. It was good I'd double-checked, as the agonized man in the hospital bed bore no physical resemblance to the self-possessed, clever, good-looking young man I knew. But from the seemingly old, old man, skin stretched over bones, the familiar voice of Ed welcomed me. We talked over earlier days and the days between, leading up to this heart-wrenching encounter with a young friend dying. I never saw him alive again.

Ed had once opened his heart to me, showing me his hopes and sufferings. That first glimpse of inner pain was as astonishing as this hospital glimpse of outer pain. How connected are body and soul. Ed died years ago, but I've encountered him since, from time to time.

Some kind of trust in life, in God, died for me with him. How could the Lover of Humanity allow such suffering for his beloved children? How can one trust again, after discovering the unbearability of life? C.S. Lewis once referred to God as "the Great Vivisectionist"; in that hospital, I understood why.

Since Ed's death a newer, stronger trust has come to birth in me, but it's taken time. Our "great grief cry," as Rainer Maria Rilke calls it, is flung into the universe; is there God to answer us?

Another young man, in a different century, let out a great grief cry. He'd experienced loss (a beloved friend died at nineteen), betrayal (a group of religious people he'd trusted proved to be charlatans out for personal gain), his own weakness (at his mother's insistence, he abandoned his beloved for the sake of his career). His mother watched and worried none too patiently, praying he would come to Christ. Perhaps for him, too, trust was difficult.

Finally, after many encounters along the way, he met Christ. Realizing that accepting this ultimate encounter meant radical change, he hesitated on the brink. His heart urged him forward, but his will held him back. At last the young man, known to us as St. Augustine, took the leap.

Later, he wrote of his long wild search for God, no less beautiful because of his tangles getting there:

> Late have I loved you, O beauty ever ancient,
> ever new!
> Late have I loved you.
> You called, you shouted, and you broke
> through my deafness.
> You flashed, you shone, and you dispelled
> my blindness.
> You breathed your fragrance on me;
> I drew in breath and now I pant for you.
> I have tasted you, now I hunger and thirst
> for more.
> You touched me, and I burned for your embrace.
> ✿ *CONFESSIONS, BOOK X CHAPTER 27*

His leap into the encounter with God altered everything, including his difficult relationship with his mother, Monica. They had a remarkable encounter the summer after his conversion. Overlooking the garden, reflecting on eternal life, they seemed to ascend higher and higher through and beyond all things until together they encountered God. After the tumultuous path

On Becoming Bread

they'd traveled, through their trust in God, they encountered one another. Only a few days afterward, Monica fell into her final sickness. This mystical encounter at Ostia helped them both prepare for her death.

Trust is amazingly resilient. Even when we think we've lost it, it can flower anew.

We learn to trust in the encounter with another; we can't encounter others unless we trust. Such encounters change us forever. Through them, we can learn to love, to suffer, to die, and to be raised from the dead.

My encounter with a leper

On a visit to Belgium, someone unexpectedly crossed my path.

For Mass, I went to St. Damien Church, where I was invited down to Damien's crypt. Sensing that door led to a life-changing encounter, I paused, then followed the guide down.

Inside, a candle burned before Damien's tomb. As a child, I'd heard of the priest who, frighteningly, went to work with lepers until he became one. Here, I learned, Damien prayed to become a missionary, left Belgium at age twenty-three, and served and died on Hawaii's Molokai island, then part of an independent monarchy.

Listening, I became aware of the face looking out at me from above the tomb: pensive, ravaged. A man in shabby clerical cloak, one scarred hand resting on his knee, the other hidden in a sling. Not long after his death in 1889, two faces of Damien were presented to the world: one holy and heroic, the other false, sinful, and selfish. Which was the real Damien?

(The disciples, perhaps, had a similarly perplexing experience of Jesus. Pretender, criminal, blasphemer? Holy man, divine one?

Some proclaimed one face, some another. How to know the truth of someone?)

Damien was considered a selfless missionary who served quarantined lepers at Kalaupapa and Kalawao, brought wonderful reforms, contracted leprosy, and died faithful to and beloved by his people. But other stories circulated. In 1889, the *Sydney Herald* published a letter written by Honolulu minister Rev. Hyde, calling Damien a self-serving, boorish man who caught leprosy by sleeping with women on the island.

A remarkable response emerged from Robert Louis Stevenson, who read the letter and decided to find the true Damien. How? By going to Molokai, walking the earth Damien walked, and talking to those who knew him.

After seven days there, Stevenson wrote to Rev. Hyde, laying out the same facts but in a completely different way. In concluding Damien was a holy man, Stevenson depicts holiness—not good breeding, high education, or a pleasing personality. It's easy to slip into thinking such ideas of success are God's too.

Stevenson reconsiders many criticisms made by Hyde; for example, that Damien went to Molokai without orders—a virtue, Stevenson says, not a fault. He agrees Damien was headstrong, ignorant, not particularly popular, but he notes Damien's holiness emerged through these qualities, for he went where others wouldn't. By giving his life to the leper communities, he made public their plight, drawing the help of people who wouldn't otherwise have come and who brought the gifts he lacked (nursing, building, educating). Was he bigoted? Once, he planned to distribute a gift of money only to Catholics there, Hyde reported. Stevenson learned that a colleague remonstrated with Damien, explaining why the money should be for everyone, and finally Damien not only agreed but thanked his colleague for correcting his error.

Hyde intimated Damien contracted leprosy through sexual contact. Stevenson interviewed Molokai residents, noting that even those who disliked Damien didn't make this accusation. The well-traveled Stevenson calls Molokai, even after the reforms, the most "harrowing" place he ever visited, "a pitiful place to visit and a hell to dwell in." Even if Damien had fallen this way on that anguished island, he adds, then we, standing on safe ground, not bearing what he bore and not giving as he gave, "should be moved to tears," not judgment. Today we know what neither Hyde nor Stevenson knew: Hansen's disease is not transmitted sexually, and ninety-five percent are immune to it. Why was Damien, one of the five percent susceptible to contagion, moved to accompany these outcast, unimportant sufferers? He became like Christ by becoming like his people—even unto death, even unto unjust judgment.

Truth isn't easy, but it's real. To see truly, one might have to change where one stands, turn around (which is what "repent" means), and go places one would rather not go. In order to see truth, one might have to learn to love.

Embraced by a fast-food angel

My friend and I wanted late-night refreshment. A lengthy search uncovered one place open, a fast-food restaurant with golden arches. We thought we'd just be getting beverages; we also got a glimpse of the eternal. Serving customers, and having an absorbing conversation, were a young woman and man. As we imbibed our tea, she said loudly enough that we could hear clearly: "It's not that God doesn't talk to people. It's that we're always feeding the flesh. So the flesh gets big, and the spirit gets small and can't hear God speaking."

Hidden wisdom at the fast-food restaurant, reminding us that God does speak to us. Directly perhaps, but often indirectly, through messengers like herself. Both the Old and New

Testaments are full of God's messengers. Some are spiritual beings whom we call "angels" (from the Greek *aggelos*, "messenger"). Church doctrine about angels may seem to us modern folk quaint or a little silly. Isn't it unlikely, absurd even, the existence of invisible, ethereal beings? In the creed, we claim God as creator of "all things visible and invisible," that is, material and immaterial. Even empirical sciences are not afraid to acknowledge the existence of what can't be seen, felt, or understood by the intellect. Why should people of faith be?

Our concept of angels may be shaped more by movies than by Christian theology, but angels have a long heritage in Christian understanding. One of the most influential teachers is early-church writer Dionysius the Areopagite. He points out that scriptural images of angels are often somewhat ridiculous: beaked eagles, flaming wheels, multicolored horses. These can be readily rejected, he notes. If Scripture used nobler images (as Hollywood sometimes does)—golden figures dressed in robes of light—we might be tempted to think that's what they really are. The earthy images clearly aren't what angels are like, so we quickly recognize they're only symbols of what can't be expressed. The absurd images open us to more than we know.

Dionysius tells us the real purpose of angels is simply this: to be in communion with God. They receive the life of God and turn toward humans to share this life with us. This means they're not individualistic, nor even pragmatic. They're part of the harmony of all things. Luke's account of the angels visiting shepherds at night, filling the heavens with the good news that Christ God is born in Bethlehem, sums up who they are.

"Why don't we hear God?" the fast-food server wondered. Indeed, it's puzzling that we so often seem not to, when we glimpse through Dionysius' eyes how all creation, seen and unseen, tells of God "transcending his own transcendence" by "drawing everything into his continual embrace." The angels speak to our hearts.

On the other hand, with our ears tuned to the uncertainty, drudgery, and injustice of daily life, it's less surprising that we have trouble hearing his voice, even with all his angelic messengers carrying it to us personally. The angels themselves can close their ears (so to speak) to God's voice, as did Lucifer, "Light-Bearer," who leads humans away from God's light. The evil of Lucifer is that he contradicts his own being. (That's the effect of sin.) The angels' purpose—angels like Gabriel, Michael, and Raphael, who are named in Scripture—is to look upon God and in turn reveal him to other beings. Like us. Dionysius presents this as the harmonious ordering of things—not a pyramid of power in which the lowest serve the highest. The greater serve the lesser, and this should be our way too.

Dionysius shows we live in a universe that flows out of the Trinity and draws all creation, visible and invisible, together to know and love God in a never-ending embrace. Church teaching about angels may help us see how God draws us into his "embrace." At least, it reminds us we're not alone.

Praying for "something more"

If you're a parent of school-age children, perhaps you get those nervous school-starting feelings as much as the kids do, assisted by advertisers who start prodding weeks ahead of time. If you're not, you may remember the years when you prepared for the school year, possibly with competing feelings. Even the computer store clerk told me one Labor Day weekend not to expect my computer to be repaired any too quickly, as herds of parents were getting their kids' computers, abused over the summer, in shape for that First Day.

I may not have thought of this on my own, but a certain twelve-year-old girl made me wonder how many of us think of prayer as an essential part of preparing for big events like the start of school.

Is prayer an important dimension of life, or a delusional waste of time? I remember a Catholic high school teacher, part of a team preparing a class retreat. Somebody suggested that the plan for games, food, and more games might be improved by the addition of time for prayer and silence—time for the Holy Spirit. Unenthused, the teacher responded: "There's the Holy Spirit, and then there's reality."

Which is reality—the inner voice that guides in prayer, or the familiar touchable world that mostly seems independent and distant from that voice? I know people who are hostile to the idea of prayer. Others smile indulgently at the harmless whim that taking time for prayer, and listening in prayer, are as necessary as breathing. Others again are curious but keep their distance, as though witnessing something slightly alarming.

If there were no God, praying wouldn't make much sense. "Being Christian," said Jaime Cardinal Sin, "means living your life in such a way that, if there were no God, your life would make no sense." I used to have a long commute, which gave me plenty of reflection time. I reflected on what other commuters reflected about, and wondered how many of them—giving upwards of an hour or two every day to traveling—would think it silly to give, say, thirty minutes a day to prayer.

A twelve-year-old, unbaptized, uncatechized girl, spontaneously and simply called me to prayer. This came from a young girls' retreat at the country refuge where we invite people for respite. The girls came from families in difficult circumstances. We gave them a few days of personal attention, fresh air, summertime activities, community, and fun. They all blossomed like sunflowers, so I wasn't surprised we got exuberant thank-you cards at the end. What did surprise me was the motif that appeared in all the cards: that the most appreciated gift was the "something more" of prayer.

"Thank you for helping us to pray," began one. "Thank you for letting me cry," said another. A third, decorated with crosses, noted: "I've been to many camps before. Some were good, some were terrible. But this one WAS THE BEST" (her capital letters).

We'd told them in advance they weren't required to pray, only to respect prayer. Without being asked, they joined in the singing, wanted to read parts, and wanted to know how to reverence the chapel on entering and exiting as we did.

Why did it surprise me that they named prayer as a gift? Why shouldn't they? Isn't prayer a delight, a joy, an opportunity? Not always, of course, as anyone who's persevered in prayer will agree. Mother Teresa rarely received comfort in prayer. Thérèse of Lisieux often found prayer agonizing. No, prayer doesn't always feel like a gift. But to these girls, standing for the first time on that threshold, it was as fresh and enjoyable as the river, sunshine, and campfire.

As we prepare for big events, and prepare our children for them, we might do well to let the children guide us on just what is needed in order to be ready.

Time: enemy or friend?

Last week, my godmother, Aunt Lucy, was in the emergency room. We heard she might not have many days. How much time, nobody knew. My mother and I felt we must take time to go next day and see her. We arranged our time accordingly.

Making good time, we arrived in early afternoon. We bought parking time and searched the hospital. My aunt was in the emergency room, a volunteer informed us, but time had passed and she may have been moved. The person who knew was on her time off. We used the time to walk to emergency. Yes, my aunt was there, awaiting a bed. Meantime, we could visit.

Entering the unit where my aunt lay sleeping, we emerged out of a tightly timed world into a place with a different sort of clock. The main event here was breathing, the beat of the pulse rather than the tick of the seconds. Did we spend time there, or did we step into eternity? We took turns holding her hand and speaking to her. We prayed, one word after another, the beads now measuring our time. By the time we finished, Aunt Lucy, to our surprise, awoke. She couldn't speak. It was hard to tell what she was aware of. My mother, who has known her for sixty years, called her by name, looked deeply into her eyes, laughed, chatted. Watching them, I saw two young women just beginning life, marriage, and family.

There are times you know you are on sacred ground and can only take off your shoes. And be aware, dimly as in a mirror, that time is a curtain through which we, in our littleness, touch the greatness of eternity: our real home. How can we get there? How can this frail, flesh-bound spirit lying in an emergency bed possibly emerge whole and unbroken into limitlessness?

Time was our friend that day. We arrived in time to spend an eternal moment with our kinswoman. She stayed on Earth another ninety minutes after we left. As our clocks continued on past her last breath, what became of hers? Time ceased to hold her; is she now held in eternity?

We arrived at her bedside one step after another. We prayed one word after another. As St. Augustine reflected, humans must receive truth this way—one word after another—not all at once. It would be too much for us. God loves gently, careful not to break us apart. God creates time as a way to enter the perfect love that is our true place, the "home" where we belong—in the middle of the Trinity, the "mutual interiority of love" (says Romanian theologian Dumitru Staniloae) where the three Divine Persons dwell perfectly in love in each other's love. But how do we get there?

In time. Through time we move to where we'll be able to transcend time, as my aunt did that day. Time is given so we can move into that center of love where God awaits us. He moves and acts within history, within time, where we are, to bring us to himself. So we can receive him and be broken out of the bonds of time, which often seem our enemy.

Sometimes I unwittingly mourn lost time and let it defeat me. A word or event triggers an old loss; despair or anger, defeat, and anguish well up and I obey: snapping at the neighbor, letting my loved one go unloved, lying to someone or simply letting myself carry the old weight that bows my shoulders. What if, in the second between trigger and action, I let myself relax inside and hear the eternal urgings of love, present in this moment? What if time is a gift to help us come to life? What if eternity really is present in each moment, as my mother and I experienced in that privileged time at a deathbed?

Division
and Intimacy

Open-eyed love

Trudging along the slushy sidewalk, I kept my left hand in my pocket, eyes alert, watching for panhandlers. In the pocketed hand was a wad of fresh crisp bills. This way, I need not open my purse, but could hand over the bills easily. That was my assignment for the morning, to give $90 to a beggar on the city street. The reason for this assignment is another story, which I may tell one day.

Soon enough I saw a young man sitting by the sidewalk with his cap out. Instantly through my mind flashed the thought: "Too young—could be out working—someone else needs it more." But the assignment didn't say to decide who was deserving; it said to give cash to a stranger.

My shoulders lightened, relieved of the burden of judgment, and I held out my wad-filled hand to the young man, saying, "Here's something for you." His automatic "Thank you" was cut short by a heartfelt "O my God" as he saw what was in his hand.

He looked up and caught my eye. For a moment, the veil was torn back, and we really looked at each other. The gift of the morning was that genuine, unprotected look between another human being and me.

How rare and difficult it is for us humans to look one another in the eye. Harder, sometimes, with those we know well than with acquaintances. A reputable marriage therapist encourages couples to open their eyes. He finds that many couples kiss each other with their eyes closed, and are repelled by the idea of kissing with open eyes—not because they don't want to see the other, but because they're afraid to be seen. Often in the most intimate moments, he says, people want to hide from one another.

It's harder (though certainly not impossible) to hide when

you're looking someone directly in the eye. Look at the person you're kissing, he suggests, and show something of yourself in turn. Perhaps you'll make a connection and discover that body and soul don't have to be in two different places, isolated from each other and slowly dying. Whether in romantic relationships, or in any human encounter, it's a risky business. Much safer to relate on the outside, and keep to oneself on the inside.

Can we have any faith in love, the real love St. Paul describes as patient, kind, ever-hopeful, ever-enduring (1 Corinthians 13)? Can such love exist within marriage, or friendship, or anywhere in real life? Love is the key ingredient of the Christian faith, yet we have trouble letting it into our lives.

Ours is a culture that cultivates loneliness and lostness. It tantalizes us with romance and sexuality, calling out our heart's desire—to experience love in our lives—but providing nothing big enough to answer that desire. "Where your heart is, there will your treasure be" (Matthew 6:21). Since the human heart is a treasure, a glorious dwelling place created by God, it never will be satisfied with less than its true worth.

Yet our faith calls us to claim, even demand love in our lives, not resign ourselves to substitutes. It tells us we can learn to love. This may mean opening your eyes to see a street beggar as a person; or opening them to see your spouse more truly; or even, opening them so that another can begin to see you.

These are dangerous practices. They may initiate change. Nor will we become loving all at once. Very likely, we'll fall and need to get up again, and again, and again. Our advantage as Christians is that we have already received the gift of love in our lives: "This is love, not that we love God, but that God loves us" (1 John 4:10). When human love fails, his does not, but returns to us in infinite patience and kindness.

Called to participate
in what's humanly possible

Are New Year's resolutions still popular? Probably. Gyms are flooded with new members in January, but less crowded by March. Sometimes we make resolutions knowing we won't be perfect but committing to the walk anyway.

Several decades ago, the Catholic church resolved to work toward full communion with other Christian communities. It remains committed to this walk.

At times, we're unaware of the pain of non-communion; when we do feel it, it can be powerful. I've attended churches where I wasn't invited to receive communion. Nothing personal, just not a member. Even in a pastorally sensitive church, it's not pleasant. Unpleasant, too, is having a Christian friend accompany me to Mass but not communion. A third challenge is attending Eucharist at which the host church invites me to partake, but my own church requests I don't.

In all three cases, division among churches feels like a sharp sword. At one of the most profoundly intimate moments of Christian life—Eucharist—we hit the invisible, impenetrable wall of division. We're together, but we're not; we're one in Christ, but we're not.

Imagine if the baptized person beside you at church, not welcomed to communion, is your spouse. When you married, you entered into the communion of shared life and vocation, made possible because you both belong to Christ. What happens when the Christian couple can't share together in Christ's self-gift in the sacrament of communion?

A Catholic husband talked about inviting his Protestant wife to church. When she was treated as an outsider there, he too felt like an outsider.

Marriage calls us to what's humanly impossible: that two persons unite, neither one diminished or lost. The church gives its baptized the Eucharist to nourish us. Can the interchurch couple—both spouses baptized, but only one in full communion with the Catholic church—somehow share that gift while respecting the unhealed reality of church division?

At least, these couples feel the pain of our imperfect communion. This itself is a witness. The Second Vatican Council, reflecting on the unthinkable situation of Christian communities divided from each other, set the Roman Catholic church irrevocably on the path toward full visible unity of all Christians. In so doing, it committed all and each of its members to this work.

The path to full communion no one completely knows. Like the pilgrim, we can only make the path by walking. It begins with our participation in Christ. It's made of our joy in one another, and our desire to be with those we love. In this, the married love of the interchurch couple is not a problem but a gift. It can draw their communities closer to each other.

Communion, whether between spouses or churches, is a gift we partake in, not a task we accomplish. We can be sure it won't happen without prayer. Prayer is the water that nourishes the garden. Still today it remains difficult for Christians of divided communities to pray together, even outside Eucharist. But there are ways. An interchurch couple is prophetic by praying together at home. Christian communities, too, find ways to pray together. There's a century-old tradition, founded by Catholics, of praying together every January. Through prayer, we prepare ourselves to receive the gift we've often forgotten we need, and the resolution the Catholic church committed itself to in 1964.

We may find it hard to remember the importance of this gift and resolution; the interchurch couple may find it hard to forget. They carry the wound of sin and division like no one else, and it affects children and generations. No amount of pastoral sensitivity will take away this burden. They also carry the joy of discovering the other in Christ.

We can draw on one another, and on the power of prayer, in keeping this impossible, joyful resolution made by our church: to obey Christ's prayer "that all may be one" (John 17:21).

Dividing walls reach

"The walls that divide us don't reach all the way to heaven." So observed an Orthodox theologian, back in the early days of the ecumenical movement—the movement among Christians, including the Catholic church, to work and pray for Christian unity. It's a comforting and encouraging word, especially when we find ourselves stopped in our tracks by the dividing walls that seem so permanent and enduring, not only in Christianity but in all human existence. Those walls are hard, and they cost us. The Berlin Wall didn't reach to heaven either, but many died trying to breach it. Many, far more, have died because of the walls that crisscross the Christian community.

What is the wall that separates human from human, Christian from Christian, sister from brother? Is it as merciless and unbreakable as it seems? Can we ever find peace?

Some twenty-one times in the gospels, the word "peace" appears on the lips of Jesus. Peace, his gift. He has dissolved the wall of enmity, St. Paul tells us (Ephesians 2:14). He has brought peace. He is hailed Prince of Peace.

What meaning can this have? How can he have brought peace when conflict and violence, unmet forgiveness and bitter enmity, are so prevalent—among nations, within family homes, among and between those who bear Christ's own name?

A helpful understanding lies in the bold 1968 declaration by Pope Paul VI of January 1 as "World Day of Peace," and his eleven January peace messages given before his death in 1978. His earliest messages recall post-World War disgust with war and its effects, determination to build a new world order, and the founding of international institutions designed to change the things that incite war: "At the end of the war everyone said: Enough! Enough of what? Of everything that gives rise to the human butchery and the appalling devastation" (1971). Yet in the 1970s, conflict not only continued but grew worse. Violence became more suppressed and hidden, as in the Cold War, but it was growing nonetheless. It's as though Pope Paul wanted to call on that spirit that cried "Enough!" before it was too late, before those who had experienced the butchery forgot or were forgotten. He urged his hearers not to give up, but to work for a new way, leading not to armed truce and oppression by might, but to real protection and support of one another. Therefore, he insisted that "peace is possible," and the world ought not to resign itself to anything less.

His messages were addressed to all humans, to the people of his era. He saw peace as first of all an interior reality, a change of mentality, deep and strong enough that actions also change. Humans are dynamic, in a state of becoming; instead of becoming more cruel and warlike, they can harness their energy toward peace. He insisted that peace is creative and dynamic, a work humans can and must engage in; if they don't act, it won't happen. As he cried in his 1974 message, "peace depends on you, too."

And peace has no foundation other than justice. It's not "a lie made into a system" (1972) but stems from the recognition of the equal worth of each human person. "If you want peace, work for justice."

An underlying message is addressed specifically to Christians. Work for peace comes from knowing that all humans are my sisters and brothers. We're family, because we're children of the one whom Christ called Father. That's why peacemakers are to be called children of God (Matthew 5:9).

Peace is a human vocation. At the same time, it's a divine work, leading to life in God. Peace can be with us, as Pope Paul urges, if peace is with me, if I am just toward my neighbor and my sister. Perhaps the wall of enmity, even between Christian churches, dissolves when I no longer support it.

Dazzled by communion

One day recently, a friend was wrestling with the meaning of communion. He'd heard a homily delineating rules for the proper way to receive the host without dropping it. All very practical, my friend noted, but is that all there is to say? Doesn't communion mean more to us than rubrics?

Immediately I thought of one of my best teachers on this subject. Some time ago, I arranged a meeting with a colleague, a Protestant minister. Rick and I were clashing over a project we were involved in. I requested to meet him not at either of our offices, but at a downtown mission where I volunteered. He came for lunch at the mission, quite comfortably eating in the refectory with people who'd slept on the streets or in shelters the night before. I didn't even see him at first because he fit in so easily, chatting with folks.

After lunch, I showed Rick around the place, including its chapel. We got talking about mission, this particular mission and the church's mission, and what it meant to have communion in this chapel while breaking bread in the adjacent refectory with those who were lowly and of no account in the world. We agreed there was a connection between liturgical communion and communion with one another and with the poor. I said: "I can see

Christ in the refectory because I meet him here in the chapel." Rick said: "I can see Christ in the chapel because I meet him in the refectory."

After that, our work conflict dissolved like smoke.

What does communion mean? I saw anew after talking to Rick, who'd devoted his life to service of Christ in his poor, though he and I can't receive communion together. "Communion" reflects the dazzling belief that we humans, underneath it all, are united with each other. And we're made for union with God, who's not just a reflection of ourselves, but unimaginably other than us. Being united with him allows us to be completely ourselves.

All this can be because Christ became one of us, so that we might become one with God, as the early church teachers liked to say. It's one of those staggering Christian teachings that we sometimes take lightly. I'm not sure if it's this doctrine people reject in rejecting Christianity, but if so, they deserve credit for noticing the enormity of the claim.

I remember being greeted with enthusiastic delight when I visited a Syrian church community, so happy were they to pray with someone who knows the same Christ, the same Scriptures, as they do: a stranger, yet a sister. Still, they couldn't invite me to communion. It's a joyful pain, a painful joy. Catholic teaching describes this as the "real but imperfect communion" between the Catholic Church and other Christian communions.

Communion is a profound reality, with many levels of meaning. That's why we can't just say "let's forget our differences and be together on this." Nobody has yet found a way to resolve the tragedy, to bring all Christians together without compromising the truth. We've moved toward each other, certainly, farther and faster than anyone could have foreseen. Perhaps it means we've all moved closer to Christ: back in the 1930s, Abbé Paul Couturier saw that the closer all our churches come to Christ, the closer they will be to one another.

So what's the proper way to receive and hold the host? How do we take it into our bodies with love and respect, and how do we live daily this mystery of union?

In Eucharist, wrote St. Augustine, "we become what we receive." We are to take inside ourselves and become Christ himself. One of the ways we become Christ is by becoming agents of healing among Christian communions. We receive this mission and this power of healing, too, when we receive the host. Let's not drop it.

Dreaming of intimacy

After intensive soul-searching and searing heartache, a friend of mine divorced. She aches for her children and for herself as a Catholic facing lonely solitude. A faithful person, she thought she was following the voice of love, both in getting married and in the way she tried to live her marriage. How could love have led here?

Listening to my friend's questions, wishing I had a helpful answer, I recalled a gift I once was given by an empathic priest. I met him only once, on retreat, and have never seen him since. He gave me a copy of a painting, which remained with me and still sits above my desk, entitled, "The Meeting of St. Anthony and St. Paul." (Much later, I saw the original of this painting by Sassetta hanging in Washington.) Not "the Anthony who finds things," and not Paul of Tarsus. This Anthony lived in Egypt during the third century. When he was still young, his parents died, leaving everything to him. Instead of fleeing into wealth and worldliness, as he might have done, he went the other way: he gave away everything and fled alone into the Egyptian desert. He was listening to a guiding voice.

Earlier, unknown to Anthony, a man named Paul lost his parents when only sixteen. Paul, who lived in Thebes, gave away his inheritance and entered the same desert. Paul and Anthony didn't know each other, nor did they know of each other's quests. Years later, Anthony heard that a holy man lived in the desert and set out to find him. They met not in the bustle of the marketplace, not in a pub or at a sporting event, but in the bare desert to which loss, love, and inner thirst had brought them both.

The artist painted words like "solitude" and "emptiness" with colors I never imagined they could wear. The landscape in the painting wasn't barren and terrifying, but fruitful and welcoming. The strangers met with joy, embraced, and looked at each other as though they were old friends.

These three people, the long-dead ones in the painting and the living one who gave it to me, showed me that despite our loneliness, human connection is no dream but a flesh-and-blood reality.

This is the communion of saints. We connect with people who have lived before us, carved out paths of love, and made an opening for God in the world. They did so, not by being more than human, but by being very human indeed. When I was little, I loved hearing the litany of saints sung at Easter. The names were unfamiliar but compelling, sung with such affection that I felt their beauty and longed to know the stories of these cherished people. Where did Athanasius come from? Why were Perpetua and Felicity always named together? Who was Agatha? St. Anthony was one of the names I heard and wondered about long ago, but he waited until I was ready before showing me who he is.

Historians say that St. Paul, St. Anthony, and their fellows, the first monks, "made of the desert a city," for so many gathered there. Could it be that my friend who lost so much is also at the threshold of discovering a new way to trust?

Being part of the communion of saints brings us home to ourselves and to our longing for relationship, which is also God's gift. We finally meet one another, the living and the dead. In this meeting, we find our true belonging.

       On Becoming Bread

It may not seem much help when we are trying to survive a broken relationship or worrying about our kids or our marriage. The dead may seem remote and unable to aid us, the living even more so. But the communion of saints is real and abiding. This is what we call Grace.

Faith and Faithfulness

What should I do with my life?

Some questions seem to be our companions for life. I used to think they would get answered and go away. Now I'm less surprised to hear people of twenty-five, thirty-five, forty-five, or seventy-five, asking what I'd thought was the proper concern of the fifteen-year-old: "What am I supposed to do with my life?"

The question comes in many ways, some painful, some apparently trivial. Many of us find the query interposed daily, in the form of: "What am I supposed to do today?" The hurricane of opportunities, information, desires, duties, cares, needs, doubts, thoughts, plans, and discussions can make the day seem like a series of hurried, provisional answers to the familiar question, "What am I supposed to do with my life?"

A particularly memorable posing of this question came my way while I was working at an inner-city parish. We were preparing for a special Christmas feast. Duties, details, and tasks accumulated and accelerated over those last few days before the 25th. A few days before its arrival, a man dropped in and asked if we had a place he could stay, as he had nowhere to sleep. Not wanting to start a trend we couldn't support, I hesitated. Finally, I told him he could sleep in the garage where we stored things. I hoped this arrangement would be discreet enough that we wouldn't receive similar requests. Returning to my whirlwind of duties, I largely forgot about José.

From time to time, he would drop in, pick up a coffee, and follow me around talking. It wasn't too difficult to toss back a regular "mmm, mm-hmm" while continuing to chisel items off my to-do list. The 24th was particularly hectic, with a plate of pre-celebration tasks served up on a bed of the regular day's duties. José came in early and started shadowing me, coffee in hand, chattering, while I discussed with myself the vital question, "What should I be doing today?"

God's grace: something José was saying broke through. I stopped in the middle of the room and asked him to repeat. He had found a pigeon, he explained again, wounded on the sidewalk. He'd picked it up, cared for it, and made it a nest. In the garage was a bale of straw he'd been sleeping on. He took from the bale, lining the straw nest with down from his sleeping bag. The bird had slept in the garage with him the night before.

This story stopped me completely, and brought everything into focus. Why was there a bale of straw in the garage? We would strew it on the chapel floor that night, to remind us we were stepping into the manger, the trough where Christ would be laid. There, and only there, Christmas would occur for us. Not only had José been sleeping in the straw of the manger, but he had sheltered a wounded pilgrim there.

Amid all my evident certainty that the coming of Christmas depended upon my hard work and organizational skills, the quiet truth spoke. Christ comes, lays his head in our mess, and says: "Here I am. Hold me. Carry me. Bring me forth into the world. I depend upon you. That is what you are supposed to be doing with your life. That is what you are supposed to be doing today, whichever day this is."

This shabby, smelly street person spoke these words to me. He was Christ for me that day.

If learning to bring forth God seems like a well-spent life, then I am grateful to have been taught by José how to put flesh on this task. Opportunities will come, daily. What else am I supposed to do with my life?

ON BECOMING BREAD

Just say "yes"

Have you ever said no to God? Consciously, that is, and deliberately?

A certain young woman was shocked to hear how loud her no was—a shouted, "No, I will not do this." A beloved person was leaving, a bosom friend since childhood, with no hope of return. Susan had no choice about the friend's departure; it was not in her power to change that. But, somewhat to her horror, she discovered she had three choices: to lovingly let the friend go, to hang on to her emotionally, or to stamp out the friendship. The moment she cried out, "No, I won't let her go," she knew she was choosing the third option: killing her love so as not to suffer the pain of being left. And she knew God wanted her to take the first option—to let the friend go and remain in love.

Susan's dilemma was about obedience—not a popular word. It has a ring of coercion and loss of choice. In a society for which choice has become god, we are uncomfortable with such a word. "Obedience" might suggest authoritarianism and loss of autonomy. We fear becoming docile, voiceless, and mindless.

What does it really mean to obey? For Christians, obedience is obedience to God. It has little to do with conforming, ceasing to reason, or becoming mindless. The Greek *hypakoi*, "obey," means to listen attentively and answer. One of the best ways to learn about obedience is to listen attentively to Mary's few but poignant words in the gospels.

In Luke 1, she is greeted by an angel and called "blessed." She's deeply troubled. She wonders, speaks, asks. Finally, she names herself *doula*—"slave" or "servant"—and speaks the words Jesus will echo in Gethsemane: "Let it be done in me according to your word." Hers is not an automatic, coerced, or unthinking slavery.

On the contrary, she's an active and free participant in God's work. She may not understand all that it is, or the part she will play. She listens so deeply that her own spirit is stirred up. She asks exactly what she needs to ask. Then she says yes. She gives her will; it's not taken from her.

What's behind her yes? Is it a spirit of fear and smallness, or strength and courage? There's a clue in the great song she sings (Luke 1:46–55). Here she proclaims the subversion of the world's order by God, who throws down rulers and lifts up the lowly. She rejoices in this work and her participation in it.

Our obedience to God may seem less dramatic, but it's no less subversive. For Susan, another thing happened when she cried no. She felt that Christ came and sat beside her, held her, and let her weep, as she faced a dark door marked "Pain," unable to enter. He held her tears, and her will, until she was able to turn and walk through with him.

Externally, nothing at all changed. The friend left; Susan stayed. Internally, everything was different. The iron clench in her stomach vanished. She was able to breathe. She felt big inside. What had felt like a stark, impossible, incomprehensible command became more like a revelation of truth, bringing freedom and new life.

In human relations, it's often my will or your will—like an arm wrestle, one side or the other ends up dominated. God works differently. Sometimes he works so deeply in us that it feels invasive, uncomfortable, like the dentist getting to that impacted wisdom tooth. Our wills may be impacted in layers of shame, pride, and hurt.

Mary's yes, and Susan's after it, is not a loss of will, but a giving-over of the will to God's. The result of such surrender, perhaps surprisingly, is that one's own will becomes stronger, not weaker. With Susan's yes came the surprising discovery that it was the touch of Love asking. Not demanding. Loving her into loving.

Deciding or discerning?

At a church meeting, I didn't realize the word "discernment" kept coming up until a guest leaned over to me. She's fluent in English, but it's not her first language. "What does 'discernment' mean?" she asked. I opened my mouth with a ready answer but an inward pause. It's simple enough to define, at first blush, but less simple to understand.

Christian traditions have produced many ways of discernment; it's an art, a science, a way of the cross, traversed with blood and anguish. It might seem that consulting God just makes things tough; don't our atheistic friends have an easier time? Is discernment different from decision making?

Generally, "discern" means coming to see or recognize, as in discerning a sail on the horizon. Spiritually, discernment involves learning to see as God does. "Now we see in a mirror dimly, but then face to face" (1 Corinthians 13:12). St. Augustine picks this up, saying faith means knowing now, darkly, what we shall then see directly.

So, discernment can seem like being in darkness. Once we decide to seek God's will rather than just go our own way, we commit to entering that darkness, going beyond what the senses and intellect can discover. It's the darkness of death itself. Sometimes we run away. Sometimes we're able to let ourselves be led a little further in, and our spiritual sight is strengthened.

Our saints can show us how to be in such darkness and yet witness the light.

In high school, I learned the story of Sir Thomas More, studying Robert Bolt's play about him. Thomas is a witness in discernment. He didn't seek conflict with King Henry VIII; the two men were respectful friends. Thomas looked for ways to avoid opposing the king. When he discerned that to remain silent or acquiesce with the king's plans would contravene the truth, Thomas spoke.

How did he discern God's will in extraordinarily trying circumstances? A reading of Thomas' life shows he was a man of prayer and spiritual discipline; he had well-developed spiritual muscles, and faith-filled eyes that could see God's harmony in the midst of human chaos. We don't suppose he walked perfectly with God every step of the way. But when the time came, he was able to stand in truth, as he saw it, at the price first of his possessions, then imprisonment, and finally execution. He and John Fisher, beheaded two weeks before Thomas, teach the power, and the risk, of faithful discernment.

Their witness doesn't stand alone. After Henry's death, under Catholic Queen Mary, Thomas Cranmer (Anglican Archbishop of Canterbury) was charged with treason for his defense of truth as he saw it. He recanted to avoid execution, but was still sentenced to burn at the stake. When the fire was lit, it's said, he stretched out his right hand, which had signed the recantation, saying, "Burn this hand first." His path of discernment can be respected by Catholics, just as the Church of England now honors both Thomas More and John Fisher.

God doesn't transgress our free will; but when we actively engage God's creative will in our lives, we can come to see more truly. Christ is our guide here. St. Maximos Confessor gave his life for the seemingly abstruse question of monotheletism: did Christ have only one (divine) will, or a human will also? The Sixth Ecumenical Council answered the question: Christ has two wills, divine and human, but these two wills are in complete communion with each other. That's our goal, too, that our wills be in harmony with God's.

Discernment doesn't mean we stop willing. To kill the will in a person is to kill the soul. Discernment means letting God's good will penetrate into every corner of our willful wills. Then we can follow Augustine's intensely difficult but wonderful teaching: "Love, and do as you will." For God's will is the will of love, and as we become like God, our wills too become godly.

The judgment trap

"It's hard getting to church in the city," a man remarked. "By the time you've finished judging everybody you see on the subway, you're not really in the frame of mind for church."

Why is it so difficult for us to stop judging? Even becoming aware we're doing it is a task-and-a-half. The subway man may be readier for church than most of us: he knows he's judging.

Senior devil Screwtape, writing to his junior-devil nephew Wormwood (recorded by C.S. Lewis), gives guidance on keeping Wormwood's human "patient" destined for damnation. He's scolded Wormwood for allowing the man to become Christian, a huge tactical loss to "the Enemy." Fortunately, from the devils' point of view, the man is far from unassailable in church. Screwtape writes (Letter 2): "When he gets to his pew and looks round him he sees just that selection of his neighbors whom he has hitherto avoided. You want to lean pretty heavily on those neighbors. Make his mind flit to and fro between an expression like 'the body of Christ' and the actual faces in the next pew."

Lewis understood how prone we are to judging and how easily we disguise this from ourselves. We wear judgment as tightly as the blue jeans of a rock star, till we either forget it's there or think it's part of us. Some may be more apt to judge others, some themselves.

How can we possibly pry off this second skin? A slightly unsavory analogy: it's said that body lice were once so common they were considered part of the human body. The first task wasn't to get rid of them but to see what they were. Learning to see our judgments may be depressing, but it's liberating.

One night, I met a friend for dinner. Violet discussed her woes, quickly stringing a long verbal necklace of worries. In the sunshine, it was hard to see Violet across the table. She suggested I come and sit on her shaded side. Sitting beside, instead of opposite, changed things. I started looking at what she was looking at—and feeling. Invisible! She felt invisible. I, her enlightened friend, contributed to that feeling. Instead of seeing Violet, I'd tallied her faults and virtues. She wasn't invisible—I couldn't see her precisely because I thought I could. The moment I got out of her way, Violet started to see through her difficulty.

Getting out of the judgment trap is tough. Judging is divine work. Not being God, we can't rightly judge others or ourselves, with our limited vision. But we're called to practice discernment, to help each other grow toward the good. Otherwise, our lives have no direction; we bump into each other in the dark or go round in circles.

Fortunately, Christian tradition says we shouldn't, needn't, discern on our own. A good spiritual director can readjust those tight-fitting judging jeans, or at least awaken the desire for better attire. They can sit beside, rather than opposite, and help free our true selves. God's much more convinced of our goodness than we are, and a spiritual director may be too.

St. Teresa of Ávila wrestled for years with her own vivid personality, which didn't always please others. She grappled with intense experiences, which some in her time thought diabolical, and in our time might consider psychologically disturbed. She suffered others' harsh judgment, and her own of herself. Her confessor, Francis Borgia, helped her believe her experiences were God-given. Her spiritual director, Peter of Alcántara, helped her trust and use her spiritual visions in her work of reforming and teaching.

Like Teresa, we may feel we struggle alone. Such aloneness can help us fall into judgment of self or others. Spiritual directors

On Becoming Bread

aren't easy to find (we need more, and need to promote them more), but they are worth the search. While waiting for a living one, we can spend time with those who have left written guidance, including St. Teresa.

I change with the changing sky

Marie's hands covered her face. She was weeping inside herself, her body shaking. "I know I need to let go," she cried, "but I don't know how."

Before she was fourteen, Marie already experienced violence and betrayal. She carries it like an interior mountain without realizing the weight. No wonder she can't stop clinging to the person who's been for her a life raft in the middle of the Pacific, but who is pulling her under. How can she let go of him, even though he's harming her?

Sitting there, she looks sometimes like an old woman, sometimes like the young woman she is, but often like a child—as she was when first she endured violence.

Profound childhood suffering isn't rare. Marie isn't unique in having suffered abuse before she was old enough to understand the word. Roméo Dallaire, recounting his experience of the Rwandan slaughter, tells of discovering a child in the woods there. He thought he would save this one child—even that possibility was snatched from him as the child was spirited away before his eyes. My helplessness before one girl's suffering had me nailed to the cross; Senator Dallaire, up against hundreds of thousands, says he became suicidal.

How is it we can't keep our children from harm? How can God not care better for his little ones in spite of us? His Son's birth into our world indirectly set off the massacre of innocent children. It seems every generation thereafter has been doomed to repeat, doomed to repeat.

Our faith tells us we must open our eyes to painful reality and enlist in the movement to transform it. If so, we must beware the fatal mistake of thinking failure and suffering are the whole truth. Tolkien's Denethor (*The Lord of the Rings*) became enslaved to Sauron this way. Sauron showed him (selectively) his own victories; Denethor, not looking up from where the finger of evil pointed, despaired because he didn't see beyond it.

What is beyond it? Mercy poured out in the world. Grace flowing, even in us fragile little humans, vulnerable to evil's seduction. An old poem of my uncle's: "small, frightened and weak, I change with the changing sky; one day eager and brave, the next not caring to try." Can we get beyond?

Children themselves can guide us. Back in 1917, three children claimed a victory they saw coming despite present suffering. What Lúcia, Jacinta, and Francisco saw and heard has been received with both faith and skepticism, now as a century ago when they were little. It may be impossible to "know," scientifically, just what happened at Fatima so long ago. This local devotion became universal because people were moved by and received it.

I suspect the Mother of God speaks and shows herself to all sorts of people—many of whom perhaps ignore her, explain her away, or don't risk making the story public. The three Portuguese children, like other children (and adults of childlike spirit), did risk. The rest of us do with their witness what we will.

It's true we need to grow up in our faith. Sometimes being Catholic can seem like an invitation to stay in kindergarten spiritually while becoming adults in other ways. We obey unthinkingly, or suspend our intellects as if they were at odds with faith. Such misunderstanding makes it harder for us to engage in the real spiritual work, the kind that helps us liberate children from their undeserved, heart-wrenching anguish. As we grow up, our faith needs to grow, too.

Paradoxically, we're better able to grow in faith when we cherish our childlike openness to God. We're all able to either increase the suffering of innocents or help heal and transform it. As with Marie, it seems impossible to let go of what's harmful. As with the three children, we can receive from God what we can't produce on our own. When we do, miracles may happen.

Reason and beauty

On a trip to France I had a weekend in Paris, which meant serious decisions about what to visit and what to leave out. After Notre Dame, I went to nearby Sainte Chapelle, advertised as having the best stained glass in the country. Stained glass was not a particular interest of mine, but the day was sunny and the destination close.

It's difficult to convey the glory of that thirteenth-century Gothic stone chapel. It was like walking inside a living jewel. The whole place seemed made of glorious stained glass. Each window told a radiant story, or many stories, of God's presence on earth and earthly beings present to God. We visitors felt lit up and transcendent.

The place was built by Louis IX as a reliquary, to house bits of Christ's cross and crown of thorns. During the Revolution, it suffered considerably; at one point the stained glass was removed to storage and the chapel used to warehouse state archives. As so often happens, God's love was submerged by politics and the human desire to be in control. I imagined those windows, and the stories they told, shut up in a dark space, silenced, for it was the touch of sunlight that made them eloquent.

What a symbol. The revolutionaries replaced revered things with state records, in keeping with their reverence for reason.

Taking over the home of the symbols of Christ's suffering for humanity, they made it a home for the symbols of human order. Beauty was destroyed so that reason might be worshiped.

The image of that glorious lighted place deliberately rendered dark and plain, and the crown of thorns replaced by state archives, has stayed with me. Is the light of reason at odds with the light of faith? How does the unprovable, the spiritual, stand up against the measurable, the knowable—things that our own age so reveres?

Things of the faith—life beyond death, meaning in suffering, our own inner life—may seem "outside" reality. Paying the mortgage, keeping our bodies healthy, maintaining our systems—these are overwhelmingly real and can leave little space for anything else. The glorious, the transcendent, gets shut into dark corners of our lives, like the stained glass of Sainte Chapelle in its two-meter storage space.

In a more obscure part of nineteenth-century France, even while those windows were locked away from the light, a peasant boy was trying to achieve his dream of becoming a priest. Success was doubtful, because he had great difficulties with academic studies. He was of "average intellect" in an era that deified reason. Only a few recognized that his understanding, wisdom, and insight were extraordinary. By sheer hard work, and the help of mentors who didn't give up on him, he was able to reach ordination.

Jean-Baptiste-Marie Vianney, a tiny nowhere priest, was sent to Ars, a tiny nowhere village. This academically challenged boy, poor in worldly things, uninvolved in "real" things like economics or politics, soon became one of the most sought-after people in France. He became known as a brilliant confessor, to whom anyone could take their troubles however big or small, and they would be held and transformed. He drew people to prayer. He was a presence of compassion and insight, bringing the touch of the Spirit, healing both bodies and hearts. He spent sixteen hours daily in the confessional, as people came to him from all over France and, eventually, from other countries.

He remained simple, childlike, and transparent to God—not the qualities we associate with success, but the qualities that made people seek him out. God's own work of art, he did not allow himself to be hidden away in the dark but received the light and gave it away, transforming the ordinary into the splendid. John Vianney, the Curé d'Ars, let his faith light up the world in which he lived. There's the Holy Spirit, showing us reality in ways we never dreamed possible.

SECTION FOUR

Brokenness

A view from the Island of Tears

This summer, I visited Ellis Island, the "Golden Door/Island of Tears" by which twelve million persons sought to enter the United States between 1892 and 1954. Sailing from Italy, Russia, Poland, and other countries, many traveled steerage, like sheep. Black-and-white photographic portraits of travelers look out from the walls of the huge building, now a museum, formerly dedicated to sorting and processing the newcomers. One portrait, a beautiful young Italian with pensive eyes, reminded me of my grandmother, who came to Canada in similar circumstances at eighteen, alone, parted forever from her home and family, unable to read or write or speak English.

Remembrances by some who made the journey are recorded there. "This is my native land now," said one; "I don't ever want to see Russia again." What broke between this man and his birth country? Did that rupture somehow find healing in the new land he took as his own? Broken relationship and new life: what's the connection?

As novelist Ernest Hemingway observed, "Life breaks us all; and afterward, many are strong at the broken places."

To be human is to be in relationship; that's who we are (for we're the image of God, who is Trinity). And that means experiencing broken relationship. This is ultimately where our pain comes from, and it's where we discover our humanity. Having a relationship break in some way doesn't make us a disadvantaged minority. The effect can be that we feel isolated, odd, alien, cut off from human-ness. Yet we all go through it; in fact, we're born into it. By the time we come to birth, our personhood has already been called into question. There's not a second in our lives when such a disconnec-tion isn't put upon us somehow—from zygote and fetus (socially considered a non-being) to old age, there is no escape. We're constantly trying to heal and establish relationship with others.

In response, we can become "comfortably numb" (to quote Pink Floyd), or medicate, or act out. If we don't face it, eventually it will face us. Some people might seem successful at keeping torn relationship at bay. Others may be open to healing, and that's where mercy comes.

And vocation comes here too. Within the experience of hurt relationship, we may discover God's desire for our life. It's not God who rejects or hates us when our relationship tears, but we who don't accept each other; that's the effect of sin. Where we've experienced such brokenness, we've experienced the sin of the world. It's not a matter of placing blame, but the reality we all partake in. That's partly why it's painful. And why the healing that comes from there doesn't just "fix" us but brings abundant life. As we enter the broken places, and receive the place where love has wounded us, from that wound comes a new love. It's why we kiss the wounds of Christ, not to glorify suffering, but to rejoice in the love that teaches us how to be broken.

On the first Easter morning, Mary Magdalene went into the depths of night carrying the ointment for meeting death. In this, she is the icon of suffering humanity, coming out to meet a broken body, a dead dream, a severed relationship. When she gets there, she finds what she couldn't have expected: not only unlooked-for healing but life beyond death, her own true name and vocation. Met and named at the tomb by the wounded and risen Christ, she becomes an apostle, witness of the resurrection.

What is broken in us, and how can it find healing? Mary Magdalene's story asks: What is the ointment for our broken places? Whether it's a breakage between persons, or within nations (as with the Russian-American who landed at Ellis), or in the many ways humans reject one another. To take on this new question is to be engaged in the deepest part of being alive. It's the work of Christ.

View from the hospital corridor

Self-loathing.

Am I, underneath all I have and have done, worth anything at all? Or is my secret suspicion true, that I'm really nothing? Nothing good, anyway.

Doing pastoral work, I found this question lurking in the hearts of a surprising number of people—including people we might readily consider better, smarter, or better-off than ourselves. Next time you walk down the street, imagine those you see having a huge rock on top of their head or great bulging sacks hanging from each hand, and you may apprehend more than your eyes can see.

I once saw a Rodin sculpture entitled "The Fallen Caryatid." Caryatids are statues of mythical, powerful, beautiful women standing casually as the pillars holding up ancient buildings. Their hands behind their back show it's easy to bear this enormous weight. Rodin's sculpture is a caryatid crumpled on the ground, sad face looking down. Aching and weary as she is, the burden remains on her shoulder. She's unable to put it down, even in her fallenness. Is she the image of humanity?

Recently, I mentioned this image to a parish youth group. The youth understood. They agreed that each of us carries a burden and, for many, it's a sense of worthlessness. They mentioned another load they commonly perceive. It runs like this: "I can do it all myself. There's no God to rely on, and I'm powerful and independent, so I'll be accomplishing everything and doing it on my own." I could imagine many crumpled-up caryatids bearing that one.

As I began to see the invisible burdens, I discovered that early-church writers liked to refer to the church as a "hospital." What an illuminating image.

Growing up, I had many images of the church. It was a social center, a family place, a house of prayer; sometimes a tedious duty, or exotic pageantry; at times a place of light and music, at times somber and difficult. As a young adult, I saw the church as the tiny remnant, for most people my age had abandoned it. As a pastoral worker, I discovered a common, though unnamed, image was the church as prison—not necessarily an unpleasant prison—where one served out a life sentence to fulfill the law. I hadn't given much thought to such images until I discovered the hospital one.

Hospitals have changed over two thousand years, but their purpose remains to care for the sick and wounded. If that's what the church is, then what are its members? Not guilty people needing punishment, but ill or hurt people needing to be tended—those weary, heavily laden caryatids—in a place of succor and healing. The primary events here aren't judgment and sentencing but diagnosis and treatment. What a difference.

Consider the scriptural image of the prodigal son. There's a liminal moment at which the young man, having spurned everything his father was about and pursued self-interest, ends up with less than nothing, despised and outcast. This story should end in despair or death. Instead, the son somehow turns around—literally turns from the trajectory of sickness and decay, completely misunderstanding the world, "mistaking less and less for more and more" (in Augustine's words). Lower than the lowest point imaginable, the son turns and begins the long road back toward home. Why? How? What happened at this moment of utter worthlessness—that empty place in every human heart?

The answer's in the parable. It wasn't judgment that soothed the depths of that weary heart. The transformer was the boundless love of the one he'd betrayed, longing for him, searching for him, as God longed for Adam walking in the cool of the evening garden.

All healers in the world are only agents of the divine Physician who welcomes us to health and wholeness. He doesn't stop to ask what we're worth. It may be our question for each other, but God's question comes from the lips of Christ: "Do you want to be made well?"

Avoid the detour

How can I help? The question lurks everywhere, ubiquitous with suffering.

The world is tilted—a few at the rich end, a multitude at the poor end. Everyone knows, and still it doesn't change. Don't people want to help? Or are they unable?

Recently, a sixteen-year-old let go his fury. He'd been raging a long time: repeated arrests, failure in school. Childhood traumas had erected mountains he couldn't scale. Family and professionals tried and failed. Why couldn't love help?

On the large scale and the small, the same perplexing question.

Christianity's response, unchanging for two millennia, is simply this. Become one with one another, by becoming one with Christ. Not too practical. But once we make that change, the practicalities flow.

Back in the fifth century, Augustine of Hippo probed these questions. Augustine was a brilliant thinker of the Western church, his influence unequaled, often misinterpreted with harmful effects. A spiritual and a practical man, he lived through events as shattering as the sacking of Rome in 410. With age, his optimism about human goodness dwindled drastically, as he increasingly witnessed human depravity. Yet he believed the image of God in us is never eradicated, though it may become tarnished, scarred, almost invisible. We have the capacity to participate in the life of the Trinity. For him, the Trinity isn't just a devotion but the heart of Christian revelation.

Augustine wrote about the soul that's lost its way, "running after less and less, mistaking it for more and more." It's what happens, he thought, when we mistake lesser beauties for ultimate reality and fail to see God's presence shining through them. This leads us on an endless, hopeless detour. We become weak, miserable, and suffering, unable to diagnose or stop our illness. We know there are higher things but can't get to them. We know there's God but don't know to find him. It's humanity's despair.

Unless there's Christ. Christ becomes one of us, pitches his tent among us, and shares our suffering. Unceasingly his love calls us until the day we can turn and run toward him. When we do (through baptism), our soul is cured; but the cure is only the beginning. We must let the cure work its way into all our parts, in preparation for the final cure, the ultimate union with God when we behold him face-to-face after death.

What can Augustine teach 1,500 years later? He teaches how God gives himself to humanity, and therefore how we are to give. Helping others involves being with them, becoming in some way one with them—as Christ became one with us. Do we want to help the poor? We discover our own poverty. Do we want to help the suffering? We enter our own suffering. This teaches us what practical steps to take.

I once lived a month with abandoned children and single mothers at Pro Vita, a pro-life community in Romania. The locals shared their lives, and at times their small homes, with the kids and moms. Without electricity, running water, or transportation, I entered a little into the community's reality—very little, for I had a plane ticket home. I remember the day a shiny green car sped along the dirt road and into the compound where we were having lunch outside with the kids (thin soup with cooked corn mush, their standard meal). Well-dressed North Americans spilled out with candy and toys, wielding fancy cameras the children were in awe of. Soon the shiny car sped away. I don't know their story; likely they were raising needed funds for the orphanage. But I felt sad they didn't pitch their tents there a little longer, at least to break bread with the children.

God's law is love and his gospel is peace. We're asked to learn the way of love, together, making mistakes along the way, again and again. We have a lifetime to learn and a patient, merciful Physician who knows how to heal.

Who's right and who's wrong?

In a retreat I led, we talked about healing broken relationships: not figuring out who's right and who's wrong, but letting new life come out of broken places. Still, we want to sort out what we're responsible for and what we're not. What needs to be let go of? It's almost never what you think.

After this discussion, I was in the garden weeding, during free time after lunch. A participant was on the porch changing a diaper. She lingered, enjoying the beauty of the woods, the sunshine, others' presence. She broke the long silence by asking me, across the garden: "But how do I let go?"

Did I say it aloud, or only think it loudly? "You're doing it! Or you wouldn't be here, and wouldn't have asked." How do we let go? We don't even know what we're clinging to.

We have help in Mary. As Caryll Houselander observed, Mary is a unique saint in having no "charism." Mary is a witness, not by doing this or that, but by being the one thing necessary for us all: bearer of God. Allowing God to be present within her, she lets go of all else. She's "wider than the heavens," as the ancients have it, for her "Yes" creates an opening where God gets in, and we get out of our prisons into the limitlessness of love.

Can we, too, become bearers of God? When this happens, we may no longer have to force ourselves to let go. We may find ourselves emerging into the wide open places, our hands empty, upraised and free.

But it's not easy.

Last week, I was in one of the world's great wide-open places, a world-renowned natural splendor, where beauty, majesty, mystery are so huge you'd think they'd be unignorable. Yet not five minutes'-walk away are streets crowded with bustle and commerce. Wafts of cooled air, a barrage of sound and activity, emerge from shops, arcades, amusements, concessions, occupying every square meter. Just beyond are huge gambling casinos under giant flashing lights.

Our inventions almost silence Niagara Falls! From this vantage point, the Falls are small and distant, just an insignificant detail.

The scene contrasted remarkably with a visit to Victoria Falls, Zambia. Too magnificent to take in, the Falls are allowed simply to be there. No concessions; no neon, loudspeakers, or amusements. A few outdoor booths offer local wares, but as night falls the selling stops, with no artificial lights to shop by. And so the lunar rainbow can be seen luminous over the Falls.

In our part of the world, we've created a cloak of noise to protect ourselves from such majesty. It doesn't completely work, though. As you walk up the Niagara River toward the Falls, on your left is this natural splendor hinting God's unimaginable splendor. On your right are myriad humans, the image and likeness of God. You can hear a thousand languages spoken, see children of all colors playing or quarreling, feel the lives of an astonishing array of humans. They're also shot through with confusion, violence, and despair. Years ago, a family friend carried with her to these Falls her own inescapable inner pain and leapt with it into the rushing water. We can't avoid forever that kind of darkness and its apparent power over us.

Becoming aware of God's glory within and without doesn't mean avoiding darkness. The Mother of God teaches to let go into the dark places. In the shadow of the Spirit, God takes flesh

ON BECOMING BREAD

within her. We treasure the image of God as light, but also as letting go into divine darkness.

It's understandable that we'd want to manufacture noise and light, because we're not big enough yet to bear God's glory. With Mary, we can let God overshadow us, allowing ourselves to let go and be made wider than the heavens. We needn't wait; it can happen while we're changing diapers.

Enslaved in our search for freedom

One Sunday morning, I was leaving the hospital. A woman sitting in the foyer smiled pleasantly but a bit anxiously, white hair framing a friendly face. She'd finished her appointment and wondered when the bus would come to take her to the mall. I offered her a ride.

We chatted on the way. I'd been visiting my father. "Fathers are important," she observed, adding she knew because she'd lost hers when she was five years old—eighty-one years ago. He and a friend had drowned. At my expressions of sympathy, she replied: "He shouldn't have been drinking. Alcohol is like that."

Driving away, I marveled at the impact of that one man's addiction, how her life and her family's had been marked by a near-century-old story still so fresh and near to her. This chance encounter—with a random person revealing a deep suffering arising from addiction—is not exceptional. Chat with the next three strangers you meet, encourage them to speak, and see how long it takes before they get to a story of addiction and how its threads have tangled up their lives.

Some say addiction is a social disease, even an epidemic. I

wonder if it's actually one of the crucial pillars that keep our social edifice erect. We seem comfortable with addiction as a permanent aspect of society. Have we given up hope for real change, opting instead for finding new ways of coping with hell? Have we become more willing to live with addiction than seek freedom?

St. Augustine describes in painfully vivid language the anguish of losing a beloved friend, who died when both were nineteen: "At this sorrow my heart was utterly darkened, and whatever I looked upon was death...My eyes sought him everywhere, but he was not granted them; and I hated all places because he was not in them" (*Confessions*, Book IV, Chapter 6). At a certain point, he notes, he was so wedded to his grief that if he'd been offered the choice of having the friend back and losing the grief, he'd have refused. You might say he had become addicted to his grief. It seems even his original attachment to his friend had something of addiction in it (though Augustine doesn't use this language), because he'd put the friend where God should be.

Addiction, in essence, is anything we put in God's place. It's whatever enslaves our desire, says the late Gerald May. Chasing after what enslaves us, we lose what we really desire—God's presence.

That's why addiction is such a trap. Only God can save. Yet we turn to other things for salvation, and when they don't provide it, we increase the dosage. Only God can receive our adoration. Yet we adore money, alcohol, sex, gambling, or work, laying down our lives for them, and we are frustrated when they don't lead to fulfillment. Feeling more trapped than ever, we use them more and more, trying to get out, and then we feel more trapped: the cycle of addiction. Needing freedom, we become slaves. Is there a way out of this same pattern, at work everywhere?

Once again, we turn to the unique saintliness of Mary, which is simply this: she bears God. That's all. Nothing comes between her and the love of God. She does not fall into the trap of addiction—of loving somebody or something, even her son, the way only God can be loved. She lets everything else go so that she can carry God.

Here, mysterious and wonderful, is the only answer to addiction. Let go of everything else and carry God. It's almost too simple to accept. And difficult to apply to daily life; knowing this answer is one thing, attaining it is another. I suspect we can't know how to do it unless we work it out together.

"Like the deer that yearns for running streams, my soul yearns for you, my God" (Psalm 42).

Body and Soul

From valentines to godliness

Anne is a pretty blonde. She always has men interested in her. She is a generous, good-hearted person; she has friends, intelligence, and a good career. How surprising to hear she finds her good looks a point of difficulty. She's learned that often people are interested in her body but not the rest of her; underneath her popularity she has trouble finding self-worth. So though she takes good care of her body, she's not on good terms with it.

Jenny has a body that seems always to be against her. It's had one illness after another, and the many medical interventions she's undergone have cost her too. Visiting her in hospital, I realized the difference between being in my healthy body, and her ravaged one; between getting along with one's body, and having it constantly fighting you, demanding, getting in the way.

If I asked Jenny, or Anne, whether they need to be reconciled with their bodies, they may not understand. If I said, "Do you like your body?" I'm sure they'd cry, "No!" What if I invited them to love their bodies? It's a hard question, whether we have stunning bodies or suffering ones. Likely without realizing it, we seem quickly to slide into either worshiping our bodies, or battling them.

The other day, I entered a shop looking for gift wrap and headed toward a shiny aisle. Everything was red and heart-shaped, filling shelves from top to bottom on both sides of the aisle, as far as the eye could see. I'd wandered accidentally into Valentine's Day, the strange annual festival of relationship. Is it surprising the shelves get filled this way? Is this shiny attention-getter filling a void left by us Christians? Society tends to the extreme of worshiping the body—manifest in many ways, from advertising to sexual norms, to big-budget pornography, which entraps many. What have Christians to say in return? What can we witness about loving the body without worshiping it, living our sexuality as gift of God without being harmed or harmful?

In the twentieth century, a movement arose to bring body and sexuality into the open, baring these physical realities rather than covering them with shame (think of Masters and Johnson or Alex Comfort). Yet we don't live in Paradise, where Adam and Eve could be naked and unashamed. Perhaps our sexuality needs to be covered, not by shame but by reverence. At the same time, our young people, living in a body-obsessed, material-obsessed society, need a word from us. They need more than just "wait until marriage."

Over the centuries, Christianity has been interpreted as being anti-body, anti-sex. At times, it's had trouble not being so. Movements have continually cropped up in the church, from the second-century Encratites on down, teaching that salvation means being freed of the body. Sometimes Christians have been encouraged to live as though sexuality itself was sinful, or the body to be shunned. This is a misunderstanding of asceticism. For Christianity, the body is created good by God, and salvation is about body as well as soul. It must be so for followers of Christ, God's Word made flesh, the person who unites in himself divine and human, whose resurrection in the flesh is the turning point of our faith.

Body and sexuality actually can point us toward God, and toward our human destiny: union with the divine Trinity. For the body is caught up into the greater yet connected reality of soul, made in God's image.

How can we love our bodies? We can start by wrestling with the corresponding question, posed by the church: "How can we give bodily love?" Christianity is profoundly mystical, but also terribly physical. It invites us to encounter more deeply our own bodies, so we might enter more deeply into the spiritual.

Take heart of a different sort. To follow this path with our lives can be searingly arduous. And searingly glorious.

Of divinity and cocktail parties

Questions of faith come up in the most unchurchly ways and places. You might be at a cocktail party making small talk, or in a bus waiting for your stop, and hear profound spiritual questions slipping in and out amidst the surrounding dialogue. As my mentor liked to say, God is not really hard to find; "he's everywhere."

In my practice as a psychotherapist, faith questions surface unsought, in their time and way. Given the time and space, people are generally eager to talk about them. We suffer from carrying them alone, without help to probe and learn from them. Daily life vibrates with faith questions.

For instance, a young woman whose parents are of different faiths told me about her search for religion. She didn't come intending to talk about religion, but because of a life trauma. As we investigated that trauma, she asked about Christ's divinity. She respects religion, she said, has faith in God, feels comfortable in churches, and could see herself becoming Christian, but holds back because "Christians keep saying Jesus is God. How could a human be God? Isn't that idolatry?"

Many stay out of the church, but few give such a profound theological reason as this young woman. Plenty of Christians don't approach so close to the heart of Christianity. It's sad our questions often go unexpressed or unmet, since Christianity is well equipped to meet them right where they're asked.

One of the earliest Christian writers, St. Ignatius, is a spiritual treasure. He's compelling because his writings are alive with faith questions, wrung from the sinews of life. He shares his reflections with fellow Christians, not academically but urgently, as one whose life is shaped by the answers.

We have seven letters Ignatius wrote around the year 108; late New Testament writings were, perhaps, still being completed at this time. His letters are dynamic, vital, at times densely theological, practical, or pastoral. Here was theology lived in ordinary lives—faith put to the test. His relationship with God wasn't limited to the conceptual; he gave everything he had for it.

Scholars debate, but these letters are generally accepted as authentic. Ignatius was bishop of Antioch, a great ancient city in southern, modern-day Turkey. Under the emperor Trajan (98–117), many professing Christianity were arrested and sentenced to be given to wild beasts in the Roman arena. Ignatius was taken from Antioch to Rome, a journey of over a thousand miles, for this purpose. Along the way, he wrote letters to six Christian churches and one fellow bishop. He called his journey to death in Rome a journey to life, because through it he moved closer to God. Above all he desires union with the divine, and for him the way is Christ. The lesser suffering is torture and death; the greater suffering is separation from God.

Ignatius begs the churches not to try to free him (Roman citizens had power to intervene in some circumstances). He's not advocating suffering and death as good things in themselves, as though one could reach God by denying life. Rather, having turned to face his particular way, he wants to follow it to the end; "every wound is not healed with the same remedy," he writes. Ignatius staked his life on the conviction that encountering Christ is encountering God. In the process, Ignatius took up his own humanity.

For a troubled, perplexed world, Christianity shows not what we "ought to do" but who we are and what's going on inside us. We're made for union with God. That's our story. Our pain is the pain of being separate from God, and not fully participating in the life of the Trinity, our true home.

Christianity's startling claim upsets our idea of God and ourselves, as the questioning young woman noticed. Can a human be

ON BECOMING BREAD

united with God? Christianity ringingly replies: Yes! Come this way, and you'll see for yourself. Keep asking, with your mind, your heart, and your life.

Why is body so soul?

> "If a man comes to me in confession and says he cannot care for his children properly because of his low wages, it is not enough for me to tell him to say his rosary and offer it up. To be apostolic, I must do what I can to have his wages raised."
>
> ✺ BISHOP F.A. MARROCCO, 1951 (QUOTED IN *THE LIGHT FROM ONE CANDLE*, BY RITA LARSEN, 2002)

One evening, Laura passed by a church on her way to kill herself. The church was offering a neighborhood meal, as it often did. Joe, standing on the front porch, called out, "Hi Laura, are you coming for supper?" As she explained afterward, the astonishing fact that someone remembered her name and face and invited her in changed her life. She went in for supper, and her life was saved.

Joe didn't, at that moment, invite Laura to confession or to Mass, but he extended the most Christian of invitations by welcoming her to supper. In his offer of physical sustenance, he answered a spiritual need too. Can we expect people to experience the Eucharist if they don't know what a meal is? Can we care for the soul but ignore the body?

It's the Christian heresy that won't go away: that the soul needs to get free of the body. We worry about the opposite danger—that we'll live only on the physical level and never get to the spiritual. In practice, that danger is more easily recognized and weeded out than the danger of making us into bodiless spirits.

My uncle, Bishop Marrocco, was a man of prayer and insight, well-read in doctrine and theology, able to convey church teaching to both laypeople and non-church people. To him, it was obvious that being a Christian meant working to improve people's lives, both immediately and systemically. Responding spiritually meant responding practically.

Are we quicker to say "I'll pray for you" or engage in issues like welfare and the minimum wage? Do we see the two as intimately connected with each other? Pope Leo XIII did. He helped give us the eight-hour work day and the church's commitment to actively promote justice, including decent working conditions for everyone. Every pope since has applied in his own day Leo's visionary 1891 encyclical, *Rerum novarum*.

In North America, where disembodied spirituality seems rampant, we commemorate eight Jesuits who lived and died with the Huron people (October 19, September 26). They understood. Father Jean de Brébeuf's down-to-earth rules on interacting with the Hurons demonstrate that the body, the material, is the medium of Christian witness. "You must have a sincere affection for the Huron," he wrote, "looking upon them as ransomed by the blood of the Son of God, and as our brethren with whom we are to pass the rest of our lives." He gives guidelines on living with them respectfully, not as angels but as human beings, from "Be careful not to annoy anyone in the canoe with your hat; it would be better to take your night cap," to "It is well at first to take everything they offer, although you may not be able to eat it at all." Love is learned not outside our material lives, but within them, in our own messy world. For Christians, salvation doesn't mean the spirit freed from the body. This is a Gnostic belief.

Joe lived the Eucharist by stepping into Laura's life and inviting her in to a meal. The Jesuits and the Hurons lived the Eucharist by canoeing, eating, working, and ultimately dying with each other. Maybe one day the church will remember to canonize a Huron or two.

We sometimes forget that Eucharist is at once deeply spiritual and intimately physical. This is true of the church's entire sacramental life, one of its greatest gifts to its people. All the sacraments carry with them a command to change the world into what they witness: the reconciliation of spirit and matter.

Do bodies go to heaven?

My friend Eleanor and I went to the garden show, exploring how things of the earth grow and flourish. Eleanor, who's been ill, was wondering about the resurrection of the body.

I'd recently attended a funeral where the prayers rejoiced in the dead man's liberation from the body and his soul's freedom through all eternity, no longer weighed down by matter. I remarked that this faith was attractive, with its sense of the soul's beauty and perpetual progress, but different from Christian faith, for which bodily resurrection is fundamental. Eleanor said: "That's right, we say in the creed we believe in the resurrection of the body. But what could that mean?"

My father, himself wrestling with questions of life and death, was chatting with my mother, and the same question arose. Half-jokingly, he said, "How's God going to do that? Where will he put us all? Maybe that's what all those empty planets are for."

Throughout its history, Christianity has been tempted by the belief that the spiritual is good and eternal, but the material is temporary, unimportant, even bad. We see this in docetism (Jesus' human body was only a kind of cloak he put on and took off again) and gnosticism (a complex system that saw salvation as the soul's liberation from matter). It's an idea many of us hold, without necessarily stopping to think about it.

Theologically, the church has always ultimately rejected such beliefs, though in practice it's been hard to shake the notion. Many communities and movements have arisen that, one way or another, feed the soul at the body's expense. Christian notions of celibacy and marriage haven't always been free from thinking the soul comes to God only by rejecting the body, with its pleasures, desires, and pains; that our spiritual selves are good in God's eyes, whereas our bodily selves are at best tolerated and at worst punished. Our society's exaltation of the body, what it can do, the pleasures it can know, is in part a reaction to this view.

Life isn't "for" the soul and "against" the body, as though they were mutually exclusive goods. God meets us in both, and especially in their union. What would change if we loved and respected the body (not idolizing or disdaining it) as beloved by God and destined for eternal life?

Are our bodies on speaking terms with our souls? Can we even imagine our bodies glorified, beautiful without the pain, touched by eternity, particularly if our body has been a place of great suffering, or another's body has inflicted great suffering? The other day, I noticed the face of a woman absorbed in listening to her dance instructor. Her skin was glistening, her eyes dancing and shining. Her soul illumined her body like a flame; she was lit up, transfigured. Her teacher's face was equally alive. I seemed to glimpse how the risen body might look, when pain and death fall away leaving only joy and beauty. Such glimpses are flung everywhere around us.

In the Scriptures, we read stories of Jesus meeting friends after his death. He feeds their bodies and eats with them. They recognize him but find him different. He carries in his flesh the wounds by which he died, yet these are changed too, no longer marks of pain but now of glory. His body died but came to new life beyond death. The empty tomb is crucial. If Christ is not raised, we are the most pitiable of people (1 Corinthians 15:19); if he is, then he's revealing our destiny.

It's hard for anybody to believe. Perhaps more important than understanding intellectually is to try it on and see what happens. This affects how we treat our bodies, and each other's. It affects where we're ready to see God, and how we approach suffering and death. Ultimately, it's an Easter way of living, and what does our world need more than the real Alleluia of Easter?

Bumping into the cross

It was a beautiful, comfortable hotel, but before dawn, we heard hostile voices from the adjacent room. A woman and man were arguing. Later, I went out to get a newspaper. Down the hall rushed a weeping woman with a suitcase; she waited for the elevator, sobbing, then suddenly went back down the hallway. Loud, persistent knocking and vain cries of "I just want to get my sunglasses" were followed by her return to the elevator amidst a renewed storm of sobs. The doors opened and she was gone. It all took two minutes.

A protest came from the part of me wanting to protect the comforting illusion that everybody and everything was smiling and content. This woman was disrupting things. Beneath the fine hotel exterior—happy families having happy holidays—lurked human anguish. "All the lonely people, where do they all come from?" queried the Beatles. One might continue, "All the anguished people, where do they all belong?"

We all have a deep hunger for relationship. Sometimes we find it; often it breaks. Always it's limited by our weakness, and ultimately our mortality.

This truth is visible in our church buildings. You can't get into a church without bumping into the cross, some way or other. Some churches have one. Some have them all over the place (my brother, visiting one church, counted more than three hundred).

Either way, you can't get over, under, or around the cross. It's made of sin and failure, and it's everywhere. The odd thing about the church is not that it recognizes the cross, but that it praises it. September 14 celebrates the Triumph of the Cross—not the Shame of the Cross or the Deletion of the Cross. What could this mean? It urges us to look and see the cross among us, changed into the meeting place between love and sin. Its triumph is the victory of life over death, even in the moment when evil seemed to triumph. Love crucified is love triumphant, and stronger than sin, by God's self-gift.

That day, by the elevator, the weeping woman carried her cross past me. I didn't reach out to help carry it. Could I have offered a hand, a word, perhaps a pair of sunglasses? Would it have changed something? I don't know; I would at least have spared myself the pain of knowing I didn't try.

Later that day, I had another chance meeting, this time with two elderly couples. The husband in one couple, and the wife in the other, were brother and sister, born and raised on the Saskatchewan prairies; their lives spanned horse-and-buggy days to the internet era. Theirs weren't easy lives, but they had grown into generous, warm adults. Both told their family story: their father's sudden death leaving his pregnant wife with seven children and a family farm to care for. That tragedy and grief were as present to Eric and Lila as though it had just happened (Lila was the babe in the womb when the father she never met was taken from her). Their cross was made of broken relationship, this time not by human agency but through the ultimate enemy, death. Their suffering was never removed, over six decades. Rather it remained, becoming infused by other forces: fidelity, commitment, self-sacrifice. Both siblings told me how courageous their mother was, how close-knit their family became. Both witnessed a triumph big enough to carry and transform the pain that never left them.

The Triumph of the Cross tells us divine love has penetrated our suffering, despite our inability to accept that gift. This power is so big that we can experience it here and now, even amidst anguish, as Eric and Lila experienced it in their history. As I pray the weeping woman might experience it. To receive this power here, where sin and anguish still flourish, is to begin to receive the gift of our cross exalted by God's love.

Do we fear human touch?

One of the few times I've been seriously ill occurred in Europe. Being away from home, it took a while to find appropriate medical help, and then the pain was out of control. My mind was starting to wander down strange corridors. As I lay, finally, in a hospital awaiting doctors, my brother sat beside me and talked of this and that. The sound of his voice, the touch of his hand, anchored me and kept me from slipping away into that alternate universe.

Human touch can actually change pain. Jean Vanier, founder of the L'Arche community, said: "Touch...human touch can unlock chambers of the heart which might otherwise become a lifelong prison."

But can we touch one another?

Isn't it dangerous to touch even those we love and know, let alone the stranger? Human touch can also be a powerful agent of hurt and harm. We tend to be wary of touching or being touched. Loss of touch may be one of the greatest forms of suffering among us.

Often we fear the sufferer, especially, preferring to keep a reasonable distance. The two travelers who preceded the good Samaritan took care to pass on the other side of the road (Luke 10). He may be contagious. He may lead us into suffering. He may misinterpret our outreach and react negatively. If we do risk to touch someone, shouldn't we be armed, at least with a supply of hand sanitizer?

This fear of one another shows up in our churches, sometimes most poignantly at the sign of peace—the liturgical invitation to touch another, to be human with my fellow humans, vulnerable as I am. To be at odds with them is to be at odds with Christ; to be at peace with them is to be at peace with Christ.

The kiss of peace before communion has been part of Eucharist since as far back as we know. What price do we pay by omitting it in the name of medical health, or reducing it to a distant nod from the safety of the adjacent pew?

Not that our fellow humans aren't dangerous, intentionally or unintentionally. We're asked to offer the sign of peace, not because we're safe for each other, but because we're often not. In the gospels, Jesus frequently heals by way of touch—touching lepers, whose disease was thought to be highly contagious (cf. Matthew 8:3), the blind (Mark 8:25), the notoriously sinful (Luke 7:37), and even the dead (Luke 7:14). As in our day, these ills caused suffering not only in themselves, but also because they resulted in isolation and alienation from the community.

Not just the feared person suffers through this isolation; the fearer suffers too, perhaps more, perhaps without knowing. Healing, as Jesus healed, meant restoration to and reconciliation with the community.

Early church hymns marvel at the wonder of God held in human hands, as the divine-human child, Jesus, is held by his human mother. Jesus came into the world within a family, real humans with real human emotions, needs, and family dynamics. He was completely vulnerable, as is any baby, especially a baby in poverty. His vulnerability was held safely by his mother, but cruelly by other humans later in his life. The hands that had touched to heal were pierced, wounded, and pinned by humans. Those wounds, according to Christian tradition, don't disappear when Jesus is raised from the dead in the flesh. The wounds still marking the hands, the side, show that the wounds remain but are transformed.

In a painting of the risen Christ sitting among children, a small girl points and solemnly asks Jesus: "What happened to your hand?" As is often the case with children, her question goes directly to the heart of the matter.

Refusing the vulnerability of being human, and dependent on humans, is tempting. The one who was actually able to refuse it accepted it instead, showing us the way of life.

Suffering, Dying, and Death

Is it life-or-death?

My friend Susan was thinking about death. "What if there's nothing after?" she mused, with alarm. "I love life, with all its suffering. Life is too wonderful for it just to end in nothing. But how do I know?"

Our culture makes it easy to ignore death (up to a point). The reality of death can get lost among our flurried lives, just another "issue" we might or might not decide to put on today's to-do list.

Christianity doesn't ignore death. It teaches that death is real, irreversible, and inevitable. But death has been breached. The question "is there something after?" has been answered. We may find, like my friend Susan, that just knowing and repeating Christian teachings is not enough. Death is far too real, too big, too final, for that. It's natural to say: "Wait a minute. I can't just accept what I'm told. I need to find out for myself." But how?

One way I've found surprisingly helpful is by living. Life has overcome death. Sometimes, though, we're content with something less than full life, "living and partly living" (T.S. Eliot). What if we dive into life to find out how it could possibly overcome death? The gospels aren't concerned with telling us what it's like to die, whether there is a tunnel and bright lights, whether it's difficult or easy. They tell us life transcends death—not by erasing or ending death but by breaking into it, breaking out from it. They point us to life. "You broke the lock of the tomb," one of the early church hymns sings to Christ. He didn't end the need for tombs, but he changed the nature of them; he was so alive that death couldn't contain him. That's why St. Paul doesn't tell Christians not to grieve, but "not to grieve like those who have no hope."

Another way is by allowing ourselves to taste death's reality—not going deliberately out to find death, but ceasing to run away from it. Last year, my father prayed with us for the souls of the dead. This year, he's among them. He's crossed the line that can't be uncrossed. His death is a reality of both body and soul: the absolute stillness of his body deprived of breath; the loss of physical presence, the ear to listen, the hand to hold; the unspeakable moment of his body's descent into the earth. I miss him greatly, every day. Since then, he is present to me in surprising ways and places, ways I never knew while he remained on earth. How much better to let these things speak to me, rather than flee or spurn them.

A third way is by loving, since love is the only answer to death. Can love bring back one who has died? Not physically, nor in the clumsy, rather literal-minded spiritual sense of the Ouija-board set. Perhaps, by their love, the dead can come back to us, or come forward to be with us. Mother Teresa thought so. "If I ever become a saint," she wrote, "I will surely be one of 'darkness.' I will continually be absent from Heaven—to light the light of those in darkness on Earth." Could it be that Teresa, or our own beloved dead, might be present among us? Might their love bring them back to us? Might our love open us to a greater reality?

The church asks us to pray for our dead, and to be open to the presence among us of those who have died and are with God. At the least, we might use our liturgies, like the feast of All Souls, to help us reflect together on the questions of death and life. And perhaps we could be attentive to the presence of our own dead, who may well be eager to show us the glory in which they dwell.

How to get out of hell

Two questions have been ringing in my heart.

One came from a gentle, soft-spoken man named Allan who

suffered terribly as a child, abandoned by his parents in a country at war. A man of faith, he works hard to keep from going to hell after death, because "I've been in hell, and I don't want to go there again."

How do I get out of hell and get to God? Since hell is so prevalent on earth, it's an urgent question.

The second question came from Juanita, who's in a tough situation. Far worse than her depression and unemployment is the isolation that wraps her like a garment, keeping the light from her eyes and the smile from her lips. Somber and afraid, she feels alone on the planet, with no one to hear or understand her.

Does my anguish cut me off from the rest of humanity? Sometimes that's the far greater pain. Merely restoring people to functionality is illusory. Real healing, as the New Testament claims, returns people to themselves so they can be restored to the community. A "cure" is useless when it divides us from all others, especially in a society where suffering is considered merely gruesome, and suffering people are too.

How do I get out of my hell and get to God? How do I get out of my isolation and get communion? They are related questions, wrung from human hearts ever since Eve and Adam left paradise. They're particularly poignant amid our society's uncertainty, not so much about whether God is, but about who God is.

Here's a popular description of God: There's something special inside each of us, some spark of divine life. All things that grow and exist around us, the environment, also have some divine presence that connect us with it, and we're all connected. All these things together make up the divine, the higher power, or "God" if you will.

This is pantheism, a common view. Attractive, too. C.S. Lewis wrote that, from his earlier point of view as an atheist, two ideas of God seemed plausible, including pantheism: the divine is the sum of all that is. "The Force," in the Star Wars movies, is a modern example of pantheism and shows its appeal.

It's not, however, the way Christianity sees God. Here, God is the one who voluntarily reaches out from being into nothingness, to draw into being creatures who are not himself, though like him in some way. If all these creatures were blotted out, God would still exist, undiminished. He doesn't depend on them for being; they depend on him. Their being is given, sustained, and fulfilled by his. It's because they are connected with him that all are connected with each other.

This is the antidote Christianity offers to Juanita's isolation: the one who is truly beyond us, but not beyond our reach. Not only are we not alone in the universe, but the universe isn't alone either. That's why we can dare withdraw from the world into the aloneness of our hearts, because everything is there.

Words aren't enough for such suffering as Juanita and Allan expressed, in their different ways. Good Friday offers not words but silence: the silence of the abandoned cross, death itself; the silence of the empty tomb, the empty tabernacle; the silence of our hearts before love in the midst of evil. Entering into this silence, descending with Christ into hell, we can ask Allan's question: "how do I get out of hell and get to God?" Perhaps we don't, Allan. God reaches us in hell. Here we can claim the song of Easter night:

> Be glad, let earth be glad, as glory floods her,...
> knowing an end to gloom and darkness....
> This is the night,
> when Christ broke the prison-bars of death
> and rose victorious from the underworld....
> This is the night
> of which it is written:
> The night shall be as bright as day,
> dazzling is the night for me,
> and full of gladness.

Too comfortable with death

My friend and I were watching his daughter's hockey tournament (her team was winning). We were thinking about Robert Latimer, a man who'd been in the news that day because his request for parole was not granted. Mr. Latimer's story asks uncomfortable questions. "He was sent to prison because he killed his severely disabled daughter to end her suffering. Does he deserve censure or compassion?"

We felt compassion for all Robert must have gone through during Tracy's life and after her death. As a father, my friend empathized with the anguish of seeing a child suffer and being unable to help. Then, with a start, our thoughts bumped up against the reality of the "solution" Mr. Latimer produced, and the places it could lead if widespread.

The modifier "severely disabled" is generally included with the story. What difference does it make if we leave it out? Is it one thing to kill a daughter, and another thing to kill a severely disabled daughter? It's not only our response to killing that's in question, but our response to disability and pain. In this "advanced" society, our terrible fear of disability and pain still flares out, sometimes to horrendous effect. As with this afflicted man.

Can we be comfortable with this girl's death? We have a concern for ourselves here. Are we putting up for grabs the life of those deemed to be suffering intolerably? None of us is omitted from that possibility. (Or possibly, whose suffering is deemed intolerable for others—I don't know Mr. Latimer, and can't say whether it was his daughter's suffering or his own he could no longer bear.) Who are we becoming, individually and collectively, as we judge the relative value of human lives?

These things are happening now, in plain sight of those who

care to look, and will increase. It's inevitable, if those who hold the treasure fail to share it. We have the gospels. We know what life is for, where it comes from, and where it leads. We know all things pulse with divine energy, and to see a human person is to glimpse God, for we're made in his image. We know our suffering matters, and it's noble to seek to end suffering but it's not ours to end life, our own or another's. And that if we're silent, we put God on the cross.

If we listen to the gospels, we'll hear Christ's disciple, our leader Peter, drawn to the warmth of the fire where everybody is gathered (John 18:15-27). To be outside this circle is to be cold and alone. There he is questioned as to whether he is with Jesus who was arrested. Even as Peter claims silence and secrecy, telling the guards "I don't know the man," Jesus claims openness and truth. Even as Jesus tells the authority to ask his followers what he said, his closest follower denies ever having known him, let alone speaking his word. Peter's silence protects his life; Jesus' open words lead to suffering and death. Peter's silence works death in his heart, whereas Jesus' Word claims life so powerfully that even the grave can't hold him.

Peter's silence isn't the end of his story. Jesus draws love out of this fear. He calls Peter to care for the sheep. So Peter becomes another Christ, the good shepherd—not because he is courageous, but because he lets love come into his shame, fear, and betrayal. Truth and mercy meet.

What does compassion demand of us? How are we to respond to the suffering laid upon Tracy Latimer and her parents? Not by denying truth, but by learning true compassion.

If we fail to speak today, Christ will ask us again, more insistently, tomorrow. Yet the call is urgent, and the answer must be given today.

Put no tools in the toolbox

A murder mystery struck a deeper note with me. The movie was about people on an island holiday. Every so often, one of them would disappear, never to be seen again. They didn't know who would be taken next, or when, how, why, or where the person went; but they knew they were all subject to the mysterious phenomenon. Not so different from real life, except that in the movie, the mystery got solved.

I wonder, sometimes, how we do it: live each day as if we'll be here forever, though we all know none of us will. Often we turn our faces from death, hiding and locking it away as quickly as we can. Even funerals are getting to be out of style, as are dead bodies; frequently it's cremation, and afterward a memorial service with no body in sight.

Death is becoming one of the tools in our toolbox, one of the array of "lifestyle choices" we like to think we have. Rather than allowing us to live more graciously and less painfully, this view leaves us fearing, cautious, and constricted.

One autumn, visiting eastern Europe, I observed something different. On November 2, my companions in Lviv took me to a cemetery, a tradition for the feast of All Souls. It was a pleasant, cool day, the last leaves just parting from their trees. The cemetery was beautiful, filled with lovely trees and handsome stonework. One statue, of a young woman in flowing robes, was so lithe and graceful it left us feeling heavy and stodgy by comparison. A poem carved in the stone expressed the sorrow of her equally youthful husband. Far from exceptional, this tombstone was nestled in among many such, stretching past the limit of sight.

Most remarkably, the cemetery overflowed with the living as well as the dead. Nor were they merely jogging through or walking their dogs. Everywhere people were visiting, chatting, picnicking.

Physical death, Christianity teaches, is final and irreversible, a real, definitive change that can never be undone. Christ has conquered death. What meaning can that have for the young husband who has just lost his beautiful bride and will never live the life they anticipated together? One of the most terrible aspects of death, from the vantage point of Earth, is its remorselessness. We long, sometimes, to once again touch the hand, watch the smile, talk over the little things of the day. The dead no longer belong in our day-to-day world, where we must be, and that is one of the great divides.

In Lviv, the living and dead mingled together. Part of life as a Christian is preparing for death, which also means preparing for eternal life.

I've found, sometimes, that the dead can be more alive than us, the living. My mother suffered for years over her absence from her mother's deathbed. She and her sisters had been keeping vigil in the hospital room, as their beloved widowed mother lay dying. "Loving and beloved," they decided to write on her tombstone. They knew their mother as a strong, gentle woman of deep faith, and they'd been at her bedside ceaselessly during Holy Week. Late on Holy Saturday, exhausted, they took the nurse's advice and went away for a meal. Just as they were finishing, they received news of her death, early on the morning of Easter Sunday.

For twenty-five years, my mother carried the sorrow of leaving her mother to die alone. Then one Easter Sunday, while praying for her mother, she heard her mother's voice: "You are forgiven." I suspect that her mother had been saying these words every day of the twenty-five years. (Maybe she'd even needed to be alone with God.) My mother's tears witnessed she was now able to receive them.

"Love is strong as death," sings the Song of Songs. Love is stronger than death, claim the gospels.

We pray for the dead. Why not also listen to the dead and hear their prayers for us?

Hope, Healing, and Joy

One of my favorite things

How many times have you heard "My Favorite Things," "Do-Re-Mi," and other songs from *The Sound of Music*? Probably too many. Wonderful tunes, so familiar they're hard to hear.

My niece Clare renewed their delightfulness for me. She loves to sing along with accompanying actions. During "Sixteen Going on Seventeen," she echoes in top voice, "older and WISER!" When the children sing the good-bye song, she waves and bows, with flourish great and smile wide.

Clare was born with Down syndrome, in a culture that finds this chromosomal condition so unacceptable that up to ninety percent of babies known to have it are aborted. She has suffered from the prejudice. But she hasn't forgotten how to revel in the joys of music and dance.

Often, I've glimpsed moments of pure joy. A colleague reads a gospel passage and pauses, eyes glistening, to savor the way God's fragrance permeates our lives. A mentally ill man reads his short story to an appreciative audience, enjoying his own ability to imagine and communicate. A widow speaks tearfully of her husband; seeing her friend listening understandingly, her face lights up in elation. My mother, walking down the icy street with me arm-in-arm, relishes the fun of being out together on a cold, beautiful day.

Joy pecks through like a slit of sun in a dark forest. It may seem small compared to the vastness of suffering, but the opposite is true. Joy is infinite, powerful, intoxicating. Like Clare inviting me to dance the Ländler, it flirtatiously reaches out to tickle us and invite us to play. "But things are grim!" "I'm not worthy!" Why say no when joy comes?

And joy comes large. The first birth I witnessed showed me

"one joy dispels a thousand sorrows." Hours of labor, a room thick with tension. Then in an instant, joy was born, and the pain and anxiety were not so much gone as changed, as if they'd become part of the joy. Sorrow and suffering may seem the stronger, but put them up against joy and see how they, too, can dance with it, as if being unveiled at last. Perhaps grief is connected with gladness, sorrow with joy, suffering with glory. Could it be?

A long-ago saint says Yes. Polycarp may not be the top baby name now, but in the second century his story was everywhere. His holiness, and the delight of remembering him, aren't only about his martyrdom. It's the way, in him, light pierces the gloom. If you haven't read his story, take time for it. It isn't objective; it's written with blatant, unashamed love.

Polycarp's story occurred when Christians who wouldn't deny their faith were put to death gruesomely and publicly. One of the earliest bishops, Polycarp personally knew John the Apostle and taught the faith to great theologians such as St. Irenaeus. He helped change the story of Christian persecution to one of joy and life, assisting Christianity to become strongly and widely rooted in the empire that was bent on destroying it.

Polycarp's inner beauty transcends. He neither sought death nor ran from it. When the police came to arrest him, he invited them in for a meal and instructed them to wait while he prayed; bystanders marveled at his composure and bearing. His captors tried to find a way to avoid harming him. In the arena, he spoke boldly, claiming Christ rather than evading death. His inner spirit was witnessed by the fire that couldn't touch him, so the soldiers had to kill him with a sword.

His fellow Christians waited until the moment they could collect and hide his bones, considering even those bones full of love and joy. It's the beginning of veneration of relics, based on the sense that a person's body is filled with his spirit.

The one true power is Christ, who gives one of my favorite things: joy that can't be extinguished.

Who's hiding in your garden?

At the words of his wife, Jim shrivels inside himself and speaks thereafter in infrequent monosyllables. She thinks he is sullen.

Shawna becomes belligerent when her supervisor criticizes her, and stalks out.

Lee cracks jokes in the face of his father's reprimand, and later pummels his brother.

You may not be able to tell by observing them that they're feeling shame, each in a different way. The people they're with don't recognize the charcoal-gray cloud over them. Jim's wife shrugs at her husband's irascibility; Shawna's supervisor seeks to have her transferred; Lee's parents are exasperated at his nonchalant attitude.

We all have our ways of reacting to shame. Often it comes over us unexpectedly, unrecognized, unwelcome. The cold sweat in the stomach, the frustration or despair, may be familiar. Shame doesn't like to be exposed but stays in the shadows, and when a light is shone in its eyes, it tries to distract or harm us so as to escape observation. So Jim, instead of thinking, "I feel ashamed," might be saying to himself: "it's pointless to say anything—she'll never understand." We might go years without realizing the shadow following us is shame. Some call it "toxic shame," the one that makes us want to run and hide. Adam and Eve became ashamed they were naked. Then at the approach of their Beloved—the One who called them into being, gave them a garden to play in, and liked to walk with them in the cool of the evening—they hid themselves. Questioned, they pointed elsewhere. Adam: "Don't look at me, look at Eve." Eve: "Don't look at me, look at the serpent" (Genesis 3).

Which of us hasn't tried it? Regularly, even? Don't look at me, look at my income. Don't look at me, look at how much trouble I can cause. Don't look at me, look at the ones who failed me.

Shame can keep us running and hiding for years, without even knowing it. Whatever it was that wounded us long ago, we've learned to protect that wound by building a thick and then thicker shell around it, and burying our real selves deep inside, until we're barely accessible even to ourselves.

How can such shame ever be healed?

There's an ancient Christian story about an elderly Jewish couple, Anna and Joachim. He was a priest of the Temple in Jerusalem. One day, another priest told him he wasn't worthy to touch the holy things, because he had no children. Joachim's shame was enflamed, and he fled into the wilderness. His wife, without knowing what had happened, also fled from the shame of childlessness, running into their garden.

The difference from Adam and Eve is that this couple fled toward God, not away from him. They showed God their naked shame. According to tradition, God responded, promising them a child. Their faith is witnessed by their actions: independently, Joachim and Anna ran to the Temple in thanksgiving, meeting at the Golden Gate. Their embrace there is an icon because their child was Mary, who became mother of Christ. So Mary, in a sense, is born of their openness to let God into their shame and pain.

My parents were married for fifty-eight years, wedded on the feast of St. Anna. They didn't deliberately choose her day, but I'm thinking she chose them. Observing them, I see they have learned much about what made Anna and Joachim holy: that healing comes in our littleness, in the vulnerability with which we turn to one another before God and say, "Here I am. Come in." Even to the parts of ourselves we're ashamed of. And it comes in the love with which we receive one another's littleness.

"Listen! I am standing at the door, knocking; if you hear my voice and open the door, I will come in to you and eat with you, and you with me" (Revelation 3:20).

Breaking the lock

Craig felt the familiar exasperation, defeat, and desolation. He didn't stop to note these feelings; they remained in the background of the all-too-foreground argument with his wife.

"Nothing ever changes," he said to himself, and eventually he said it out loud, in just that contemptuous tone Julia had been expecting, with dread. "You don't change, and this so-called relationship doesn't change," she flashed back, as if from the script of one of those plays that run thirty-five years, the same dialogue repeated night after night. Theirs had run only twelve years, but both were feeling ready to shut it down forever.

What was the point? Every time you felt like you were getting somewhere, a dead end. You were back again stunned, then horrified, achingly sad, enraged.

Our circumstances differ from Craig and Julia's, but the questions lurk: Are we getting anywhere? Is there any meaning in all this? Sometimes we're disconnected from the part of our soul that is asking. If there's no answer, or the answer is no, then what?

We might ask the same of Christianity, which says Christ's presence wrought redemption. Where's the change, then, the better world? "They have taken my Lord away, and I don't know where to find him" Mary Magdalene's cry echoes in our lives (John 20:13). Our hearts may whisper: "I thought I was following God, but I've come to the place and he's not here." "I thought love would remain, but it is fled and I am desolate."

Mary Magdalene, standing in the garden before dawn at the empty tomb, is an icon for us. After she met Jesus, it seemed there was healing for her, a real work to do, companions along the way. Now she is alone after the two darkest nights in history, the nights of Death Triumphant, and hope dashed beyond hope.

ON BECOMING BREAD

Nights such as our hearts have known. Craig and Julia knew them. Sometimes each thought the other was causing them, but down deep each was sure the fault was his or her own.

Beyond the dark nights, and more terrifying: emptiness. Not simply that the Lord is dead, but that he's disappeared completely. It's the wringing emptiness that topples us when we've followed as best we can, and love has vanished, powerless.

Mary's cry brings two apostles to the tomb. They see but don't understand and return home. Mary stays, past the end of hope. Through her tears Mary sees that, as there was emptiness beyond darkness, there's something beyond emptiness too. A joy that breaks the past, breaks the heart, and breaks death itself.

Jesus says, "Mary." She recognizes him: life raised from death. With her, we learn that salvation comes to us. The garden where Mary stands is lost Eden, agonized Gethsemane, and the awaited paradise. She beholds the power of God's love and work, accomplished but not yet completed.

We may feel stuck back at the beginning, in our relationships, our lives, our church, our world. It's not a matter of getting out of here and finding life. It's a matter of life coming where we are. Mary finds an empty tomb with a broken lock and discarded cloths. Beside this tomb she meets Jesus. Though death stands between them, it cannot separate them, for in him the living God has taken flesh.

It's our story too. It can remind us we're never "right back where we were" as long as life is in us. For Mary, there's no hope in her standing in the garden unless God acts in a way that can speak through her tears. We don't have to simply accept whatever suffering comes our way and never attempt to change our lives. We must be ready to meet the resurrection.

Mary Magdalene has for two millennia been named "equal to the apostles." She witnessed the resurrection, as can each of us. We don't have to do it alone.

Why carry rocks around?

Long ago, I let a friend down. It's still vivid in my memory. At the last minute I canceled, leaving her in the lurch. She was cold and angry on the phone, and we hung up quickly. I couldn't blame her; I'd hurt her. Though I apologized, the effects remained.

I don't know what happened with her, because she stopped speaking to me. But for me, a burden was created that I long carried: guilt. Part of me was reluctant to put it down, as though staggering under it would gain me points, and enough collected points would earn me forgiveness. This type of guilt, someone observed to me, is like a knapsack full of rocks strapped to one's back: a dead weight that gradually, increasingly, wearies the bearer.

In the movie *The Mission*, Rodrigo kills his brother. Assisted by Fr. Gabriel, he turns to Christ and accompanies the Jesuits in their mission work. Rodrigo chooses a penance: climbing with the Jesuits up the rock cliff of Iguazu Falls, dragging a sack filled with his armor and weapons. A strong man, he suffers immensely bearing the weighted sack. Finally, one of the brothers tells Fr. Gabriel he thinks Rodrigo has done this penance long enough. "*He* doesn't think so, John," replies the priest. "Until he does, neither do I."

How many of us carry a sackful of rocks, weapons, or armor? Do we feel a fitting punishment will somehow earn us salvation? Such thinking is a subtle inversion of the truth of mercy and repentance. Repentance brings about real change; it's a response to the experience of God's love, drawing us away from sin into life. Guilt, carried as a dead weight, can convince us we must change so God can welcome us.

Truth without mercy is like that. It shows us ourselves, sinful, deserving nothing, needing everything. It seems just and accurate, and in a sense it is. Still, it's a partial truth, which becomes a lie, for there can be no truth without mercy.

We're never asked to see our own sin except in light of God's mercy. One of the great Christian tragedies is the prevalence of the idea that we must earn love and forgiveness. Accompanying it is the loss of a sense of mercy, the healing oil that flows through our lives. Guilt may be powerful; mercy is eternal.

Mercy isn't orderly, though. It can mess up our neat categories of "good" and "bad," "righteous" and "unworthy." The Pharisee thought he was right with God and the publican sinful; he didn't know the publican was at that very moment, at the other end of the temple, opening himself to God's mercy. On another occasion, the assembled crowd was sure Zacchaeus was a bad man; they didn't know that even as he climbed a tree to see over them, his heart was turned to repentance and ready to receive God's mercy.

Likely we are indeed guilty, each of us. Guilt without mercy can keep us stuck, packed with dead-weight rocks. We may not find our churches filled to the rafters, because it's hard to turn to mercy. We associate it with guilt and punishment, and who wants that? Or maybe it's just hard to face ourselves. Whatever the reason, if we stay away from mercy we're choosing the harder path.

Mercy comes now. We're not awaiting a future event, but being opened to the mercy that flows everywhere. Life is not a matter of collecting merit points, but an invitation to drink from the well of God's love for us. Evagrius of Pontus, a fourth-century monk, says we can break away from sin only in the measure that we experience the love of God.

None of us undertakes the journey alone, yet as with Rodrigo, none can decide for another how to live it. Instead of debating whether Christ really rose from the dead, we can taste resurrection for ourselves.

SECTION EIGHT

Life

How to waste time

Just before Christmas, I spent some days at a Benedictine monastery in Quebec.

Beforehand, I wondered what exactly I was doing. The week before Christmas is a lively time in the city, with plenty of concerts, gatherings, treats, and sales. There were Christmas preparations to make. Where was I going, and for what?

With non-refundable travel tickets, it was difficult to back out. A day's journey, by several modes of transportation. I felt like a pilgrim.

It was a strange contrast. Stepping out in the city was like stepping right into a spinning, whirling top, in a mash of people, overloading the senses. Here, stepping alone out of the taxi into the dark, cold night meant losing all familiar reference points. A lighted, arched doorway was all I could see.

I was ushered directly into Vespers in the vast abbey chapel, where black-robed monks stood in quiet formation. Thirty unaccompanied voices rose as one in the chapel's stillness, singing ancient Gregorian chant in a language the world has forgotten. At that moment, still carrying the bustle of the place I'd come from, I saw the strangeness. Why were these men spending time this way? To whom were they singing? Weren't they throwing away their lives, which could be spent raising children, building bridges, designing smartphone apps, buying and selling, getting and spending...

Surprisingly, surrounding me were people of all ages, some quite young. Had their parents coerced them into coming? Later, I learned these young people were here by their own volition, not always keeping silence (intermittent whispering and hidden laughter occurred), but participating willingly.

I arranged to speak with one of the monks. He was chatty and likable, talking about people he'd met over his forty years here, asking about my life.

Finally, I came to the point. "How do we know God's will?"

He laughed. "I don't know. God is a big mystery."

He told me his experiences, how a vow of poverty led to looking after monastic finances, a vow of obedience led to having others obey him. The story of his life unfolded through decades spent in this place, among these people, in this way. "You mean you know God's will in the doing of it?" I suggested. He said, "Pray to the Holy Spirit. Pray to abandon yourself to God." At home, I may not have managed it. Here, with little else to do, surrounded by prayers of the living and the dead, it came easily.

How odd to seek self-abandonment when we're mostly told to get in control of our lives. How foolish to let go into the darkness of faith.

Prayer takes us into dangerous waters, and through them, to places we can't go if we merely follow our own strategic planning. This abbey's birth in 1912 came out of tragedy. In 1901, when Benedictine monks were driven out of France, Saint-Wandrille abbey decided to establish a new foundation in Quebec. They sent five men. The fledgling community was almost destroyed when its dynamic leader, Dom Vannier, drowned in the lake just two years after their arrival. Eventually the Canadian monastery became independent.

Having survived so much and more during these hundred years, the abbey's monks continue to sing the Psalms daily, wasting their lives praying, working, receiving guests. Thomas Merton, writing in an American Cistercian monastery during World War Two, wondered if such pockets of prayer kept humanity from blowing itself up.

Today, North America is sustained by several contemplative monasteries. Is it the voice of prayer raised there, and in the hearts of all who cry out to God, that anchors our world and gives hope amidst doubt, stress, and confusion?

And helps us to hear, deep in the veiled and lidded nooks of our heart (where we usually prefer not to go), these eternally spoken, completely personal and intimate words: "You are loved."

I can't think of a better waste of time.

Life as poetry

Jonathan was recalling conflict with a coworker. He paused a full minute, then said, "I'm not an angry person, am I? I don't want to be an angry person."

Why is it difficult to acknowledge we're angry? Even those of us who are pretty good at showing anger can find it hard to own. We might fear its power, having experience of the terrible harm anger can unleash. Yet some church fathers thought anger existed in Paradise. Could we imagine anger an unfallen, pure gift of God? A force that works within us, creatively rather than destructively?

When we let anger move properly, it can open up our spiritual lives. In this regard, the Psalms are teachers.

The Psalms are hymns. Often their poetic verses are used to express anger: at God, circumstances, people. These poems can help us meet, express, and learn from forces like anger, rather than hiding from or blindly obeying them. The Psalms show us hidden treasures.

What can whisper the Lord's mysteries like poetry? What can mend the wounded soul more profoundly? One of the oldest, richest New Testament texts is a poem (Philippians 2:1–11): "He did not regard equality to God a thing to be grasped, but emptied himself..." The church embraces the power of poetry to speak in ways prose can't. The universal church recognizes a Syrian saint, Ephrem, who used poetry to express divine truth. I love him for being an ambassador of poetry, in ways our prosaic selves can't manage.

St. Ephrem the Syrian was a monk, theologian, holy man, and poet. His hymns on Paradise, Christ's birth, the Passion, his much-repeated Lenten prayer that says it all in a few words, can reach into our dusty places and polish them to beauty.

Sometimes we get to thinking that church teaching is prosaic. Throughout Christian history, there's been a creative tension between two goods. One is the inner mystical life of each person; the other is the public, communal life of the church. Yet they need each other, and the church's poetic texts help connect them. Christianity is profoundly personal. That's why our inner selves matter, and that's what brings us into the communion of saints (the church).

The church opens us tiny humans to God's vastness. "Thy infinite gifts come to me only on these very small hands of mine," wrote the poet Tagore. Our liturgy is lived poetry. A key Easter moment is the ancient "Exsultet" poem. Our Creed proclaims belief in God the "creator"—"*poet*" in the original Greek. Poetry is powerful with the creative power of God, who speaks his Word and so creates—makes poetry. When we bring our poetry before God, we're making a dwelling place for him. Our responsibility is to make it a true dwelling.

When we no longer can hear the language of poetry, will we be able to hear God's word to us? St. John of the Cross wrote a long prose explanation of the spiritual life—but only upon request. He preferred us to read his poem, and go where it points.

As Jesuit Gerard Manley Hopkins wrote, "there lives the dearest freshness deep down things." Poetry can help us turn to God: "I live my life in ever-widening circles that reach out across the world" (Rainer Maria Rilke). It can help us face death, with poet Khalil Gibran: "The deeper that sorrow carves into your being, the more joy you can contain." It can waken us to the divine, as with medieval Arabic poet Rumi: "The breeze at dawn has secrets to tell you. Don't go back to sleep."

The language of poetry waters our hearts, especially in places where we have difficulty receiving. Such as anger. "Glory to him, who came to us by his first-born! Glory to the Silence, that spoke by his Voice. Glory to the One on high, who was seen by his Dayspring!" (St. Ephrem).

Of holiness and finesse

A woman had a problem. Her parents arranged for her to marry. It wasn't the life she wanted; she had things to do, which didn't involve marriage. Caught between duty and desire, she obeyed and got engaged.

Before they could be married, her betrothed died in an accident.

The woman, known as Macrina the Younger (324–379), lived when it was difficult for a young woman to oppose her parents or remain unmarried. They would certainly make a new marriage arrangement for her. Still, she had a desire to live her life another way. Was it willfulness or selfishness?

It was a deep connection with the Holy Spirit. She found a way to follow her heart without turning from duty. Since she'd been the man's intended wife, she declared, she couldn't marry anyone else, and so would never marry. She hadn't desired his death and didn't disobey her parents. Using her creativity and inner strength, she seized the moment, refusing all subsequent offers of marriage.

Because of her younger brother Gregory's writings, we know Macrina's story. Her solution highlights a characteristic I'd call "finesse." I've heard finesse defined as "smooth maneuvering" or "artful management." We might not associate it with holiness.

Here's another way to describe finesse. A friend took me rock-climbing. Though a rookie, I learned much, including how exhilarating the view is when you've climbed beyond your fears to get there. At one point I got stuck, unable to find a way up. My friend clambered up (oh so easily!) beyond me to scout a way. He told me to step sideways to a foothold, then sideways again, then up. Astonishingly easily, there I was up on top. When the direct path didn't work, and staying stuck was untenable, the surprise sideways move got me there.

The spiritual life is not unlike rock-climbing. We need not only strength and skill, but also finesse, to get there.

Macrina's younger brother was St. Gregory of Nyssa. She was also elder sister to St. Basil the Great. These brothers, with their friend Gregory of Nazianzus, are the three Cappadocian Fathers whose theological brilliance and personal holiness are a lynchpin of Christian tradition. Praising her creative genius, Gregory tells us they owe it all to Macrina. (There would be good reason to make her the patron saint of sisters, given her gift for bringing out the best in her brothers. My brothers should hear about her.) He portrays her as a wise philosopher, a gifted teacher, healer, and theologian, and above all, a woman who loved God.

Having found a way to remain single, Macrina continued to employ her "artful management." After her father's death, she persuaded her well-to-do mother to turn the family estate into a community house, inviting their servants to join. Together, they provided shelter, education, and healing to all in need. She did some of her best work in hidden ways. Only after her death did her famous brother learn about the many people she'd healed and the ways she'd used her gifts to build a remarkable community.

What if we faced our problems (and society's) with creativity and finesse, combined with courage and prayer, in the spirit of Macrina? We might rouse ourselves to action rather than shaking our heads at the mess. We might rediscover our sense of humor, and our boldness. We might come closer to God.

We may find, too, that God uses finesse with us. When we've no idea what's going on, except that it all seems pretty uncomfortable, we may discover he's been up to some artful management. He might use our natural curiosity and longing for "more" to help us discover the secrets of physics or biology—the inner depths of the universe he made for us. His law is love, and his love is poured out for us, everywhere.

The flame undimm'd

The church was in darkness when I came in, the Easter Vigil just beginning. Then the paschal candle was lit. Its fire was passed around the church, until many tiny candles together became a mass of light.

But there weren't quite enough candles, and a small cluster on my side of the church remained in darkness. A few came over to share their flames, saw the cluster had no candles, and returned to their seats. Finally, two came over and gave their lighted candles away to the children in the little cluster. Both children who had received lighted candles kept them lit a long, long time, well after the electric lights had been turned up.

Watching, I felt sad for the several hundred people who hadn't found a way to share the flame with those who had nothing. I felt the beauty of seeing two give away all they had, so that those with none could have light.

Maybe the hundreds didn't understand that they are light-bearers. Maybe they thought somebody else was supposed to be doing it, and didn't dare. The Easter Vigil calls us back to our baptism, giving us again the light and urging us to share it. If we don't, who will?

Sometimes it's hard to let the liturgy light the fire of our faith and stir us to action. Sometimes it's hard to relate our day-to-day lives and work to the liturgy. Yet it's in the tension between the two—our liturgical life, and our day-to-day life—that we really become Christian. We can't give up one or the other. "Liturgy," literally, means "work of the people."

In 1955, Pope Pius XII gave a way to help relate liturgy to life, instituting the feast of St. Joseph the Worker on May 1. "May Day," or International Workers' Day, had long been linked with the common worker and the call for just labor practices. With this new feast, Pope Pius showed the spiritual meaning of labor and the dignity of work. These values have been reiterated by all subsequent popes and the Second Vatican Council.

In our own day, I've seen the oppressiveness of having no proper work, feeling valueless and useless. I've seen the destructiveness of the 24/7 work mentality, infiltrating and corroding family life and relationships. At both extremes, it's our humanity that is being ground down. It's not surprising that today's church members have trouble seeing themselves as light-bearers, the frontline workers who have what their neighbors need.

Joseph the Worker gives us not a concept, but a person, to help us understand the connection between liturgy and work. Joseph, who provided for Jesus and gave him a trade, becomes the model for Christians seeking to understand their life and work. He can help employers treat their workers justly, and workers understand the value of their labor.

In North America we recognize Labor Day in September, not May, and the feast of Joseph the Worker is a bit hidden. It proclaims our dignity in the work we do, benefiting family and society and glorifying God. It reminds us we are the light-bearers.

The church's liturgy illuminates our work and relationships. It's not a one-or-the-other proposition: Joseph the husband, Joseph the servant of God, carpenter, teacher and laborer, Joseph the man of prayer and fidelity, are all one person. All we do and live in liturgy is real, not a play or pageant unrelated to life. Liturgy is the deepest expression of what our lives are about. It's food that helps us feed those beyond the walls of the church. It gives a word we can speak everywhere we go.

It's said that St. Joseph, though silent in the gospels, has excellent hearing. Through his hearing, may the "work of the people," the liturgy in which we all participate, be part of all we do. May it help us find better ways to treat one another, provide proper work, and receive one another's labor.

New Life

What is truth?

Myra was suffering profoundly. Some people blame themselves when life gets tough, taking everything inside. Some, like Myra, take everything outside, blaming everybody but themselves.

Over the past few days she had some especially hard things thrown at her. Listening, I felt distressed for her, and I felt lost, wondering what was going on. Finally, I blurted: "Myra, have you ever found truth in your life?" She looked me full in the face. "This is truth," she said clearly, "this kickback for all the bad things I've done in my life."

Myra's words were from the gut. Truth is judgment, and the judgment is: I'm guilty. I'm unworthy. It's my fault, and I deserve it.

Not everybody says it as clearly as Myra did, but I suspect many of us think that way. We slap up against the stark, irrefutable "truth" of our own failure: sharp-edged, barren like the desert under the sun. Life holds the mirror, and what can we do but agree with the judgment?

It might seem as though the church brings us back to this judgment we're trying to escape: I'm a sinner, I'm dust, and the rest is just a mask. Yet Christianity isn't about judgment, failure, and dead ends. It takes us into the desert, but not alone. It urges us to climb the mountain, but with Jesus. If we follow, we will travel from the depths to the heights, from the outside to the inside, from desert to mountain to Jerusalem, Calvary, the tomb, and all that lies beyond. "Come with me," says Jesus, "and I will take you places."

We will hear on the lips of Pontius Pilate the question Myra raised for me: "What is truth?"

The irony is that Pilate looks upon the face of Christ as he asks. Truth is not a something, a concept or idea. Truth is someone, the one with whom we've been walking, perhaps the one we've been judging, whether we know it or not. Truth is with us, and within us. Looking into the eyes of truth, Pilate asks, "What is truth?" Had he dared to act on what was within, he would have found the same truth. Perhaps the reason he didn't is because, like Myra, he feared that "the kickback for all the bad things I've done" is the real truth. How difficult it is to receive the truth that Pilate beheld without seeing, the truth that is mercy, flowing like oil.

One of my best teachers about the truth was named Peter. He rarely took a bath or changed his clothes, and he lived in the smallest apartment I've ever seen, next to the furnace. Neither his body nor his mind could earn a living for him. He ate at soup kitchens and missions or from a can in his basement. He was often cheated and sometimes swore at people who stepped on him.

The truth about Peter is that he was a man of prayer, faith, and hope. When he shone, he really shone. I saw him shine at a retreat held at a mountain outside Montreal. Gone was the unkempt, cigarette-stained street bum that city folk know how to render invisible. With people who accepted and wanted him, he was aflame. He spoke to everybody, especially the lonely. He cracked jokes, made people laugh, prayed for people out loud, set hearts at ease, and couldn't stop smiling. I saw him transfigured, as Jesus was transfigured on the mountain.

After several years knowing Peter, on that mountain retreat I glimpsed him as (I believe) he looks in heaven, where I'm sure he is now. That's the truth love and mercy can see, the truth I pray Myra might receive. That's the truth we are all asked to claim, if we let the Spirit dance us through.

Did he, or didn't he?

Did he, or didn't he? What difference does it make?

Whatever may be said about, for or against Christianity, the response will always be demanded of it, and always should be: Did he, or didn't he, rise from the dead?

I respect human ingenuity's ability to solve great puzzles. Someone may yet discover a way to decipher what happened in that empty tomb so long ago. Must we wait until technology can solve an ancient mystery?

One year, I put it to God insistently and demandingly, like a child: "Well, did you or didn't you? Before I go around telling people you did, I want proof!"

Proof in the form of lost tombs, obscure Roman records, or new ways to analyze dust did not arrive. Something else happened: I was nailed to the cross. Pinned, I couldn't run around collecting evidence; I had to look somewhere else entirely—within. Things changed. A response came to a second question I didn't realize I was asking. Not just "were you raised from the dead or not?" but also, equally urgently, "and what difference does it make?"

If Christ is raised, then I can be raised. The question is completely practical, not future and distant, but in this moment. Now I see that the question is everywhere, and many are asking it with their lives. Our death-avoiding society may have difficulty in hearing, because resurrection comes out of death.

Years later, I was sitting in prison. In the prison chapel, a young man named Ben met an older man named Joe.

I was "Just Visiting," as the Monopoly board says, assisting a program for inmates. Nobody had come to collect Joe, an inmate who'd been in a preceding program, so he stayed and chatted. I think he'd spent most of the day that way. With his wiry body and scarred face, he listened to twenty-year-old Ben tell of being in jail for the first time, awaiting trial. Joe wanted to tell his story for Ben's benefit.

Joe recounted how he had been in and out of prison for thirty years, from when he was younger than Ben. Short stays, long stays. Anger, violence, betrayal, confusion, fear, and anguish. Friends disappearing, family broken-hearted. Attempts to change, vows to never again end up inside. A terrible moment with his hands around the neck of someone he believed had wronged him, futile running, and the final clang of that prison door on him once again, this time for murder. For three days, lying on the floor of his cell, he did not move, even to eat or drink. Nothing was left.

At the end of the third day—Joe said to us—"When there was nothing, there was God."

Externally, nothing was different. Joe was still in prison, facing the same consequences. Did he, or didn't he, begin a new life that day?

He knew the answer. He'd received a new life not of his own making. Part of this new life, he said, was witnessing it to others.

I think of Joe sometimes as I stand in the emptiness into which the church invites us on Good Friday. Emptiness may be the last place we want to go, though we may not find as dramatic ways to avoid it as Joe did. Joe stands beside Mary Magdalene, in the early dawn, up against the empty tomb, not even a body left.

Joe, like Mary, had courage to proclaim the unbelievable good news. Mary Magdalene is called "equal to the apostles," because she witnessed the resurrection. Until technology unlocks the secrets of that tomb, how will any of us become apostles? We must go to the emptiness, as Mary did for one reason and Joe for another, and find out whether we are raised from the dead.

Then the Easter Alleluia will not be an awkward duty but a cry of joy springing from within. We may be surprised at how many voices are singing it together.

Would I die without the Trinity?

"I would die without the Trinity," my friend Father Peter says. How many of us would echo him? Does the Trinity make much difference to our lives or our faith? Yet it distinguishes Christianity from all world religions.

Let me give two earthly glimpses of the Trinity. They won't exactly make us understand—as Augustine said, if you think you've understood God, it's not God you've understood—but may help illuminate the question.

The first involves a table laid for a banquet. A Christmas banquet. The tables are rough, as often in soup kitchens, but carefully laid with clean white cloths, bright green napkins, and the finest red plastic glasses available. Turkey, cranberries, and potatoes are everywhere, and all the chairs are filled. The guests come from varied backgrounds, some well-dressed, some wearing worn-out t-shirts and jeans. It doesn't matter; all are welcome; all are smiling.

Especially so is Doreen, sitting at the head of one table. People tend to sit at a certain distance from her, owing to the rather strong smell of her body. She lives alone with—as is later discovered—a record number of cats. As she digs into Christmas cake, Doreen exclaims aloud: her slice contains a tiny golden crown! She is crowned Queen of Christmas! Already happy, she is now bursting with joy, transformed into a radiant flame. Her beauty is astonishing.

It's the hospitality of Abraham, who entertained angels (Genesis 18:1–8).

In Andrei Rublev's icon of this scene, three figures sit around a round table, in perfect relationship, each looking at the other, all welcoming the guest—you and me, the people gazing at the icon. On the table is a cup. The three are complete, an equilateral triangle in a circle. They are also open, waiting for us to sit with them. There is no icon of the Trinity (except us), but this icon gives a glimpse of the Trinity.

No wonder Father Peter would die without the Trinity. God is relationship. God is welcome. God is love perfect in itself, but perfectly open to receive the other. Entering in, we become who we are meant to be.

The second glimpse features a brief bus ride. As I hop on, I greet the driver. She responds pleasantly. I sit within talking distance, as nobody else is on the bus.

We discuss the weather, in true Canadian fashion. In the process, she reveals she lived in the country once. She had her three kids there, and began and ended her marriage there. Calmly enough, eyes turned away from me toward the traffic, she remarks that her youngest, only four years of age, is in anger treatment and she won't be seeing the child till he is eighteen. The two older kids, both teenagers, have problems of their own. All three were abused by their father, as was she.

All this comes out in the time it takes to drive three blocks. A crown of pain. I think about that four-year-old, sent away from both parents. But if I have any temptation to judge the mother, her final remark brings me up short. She is saying how much she misses him, and what a sacrifice it was to lose him. She feels letting him go gives him a better chance than his elder siblings had. Though she is composed, the suffering of this story is written into her body.

A woman on the cross, acting out of love as best she can. On the cross the Trinity is revealed: the relationship of love that is God. This love becomes tragic when it enters the brokenness of humanity, but it is not broken. It takes on woundedness, yet it brings healing. It's a love that turns everything upside down.

There's nothing ordinary about the power of this love that welcomes the stranger, transforms the sufferer, and calls humans to love even on the cross. Still, it's the ordinary stuff of our lives. We would die without the Trinity.

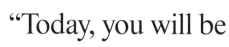

"Today, you will be with me in Paradise"

One of my best teachers was Helen.

She was a tiny woman with yellow curly hair, no teeth, a limp from a bad hip, and swollen feet. She loved to greet strangers, bake muffins for people, and help out at the breakfast club and the Mission. She smiled and laughed easily. She was a chatterer, but her chattering was generally random and disconnected, hard to follow and easily dismissed.

Indeed, she was among the easiest of people to dismiss: an old, poor, solitary woman, living on social assistance in a squalid apartment. Though a wife and mother of many, she was quite alone in the world; long separated from an abusive husband, her children taken away one by one by the Children's Aid Society. When I met her, Helen had largely left the world of sanity—with good reason, as refuge from the world which, for her, was a crazy and dangerous place.

When Helen had a stroke and was taken to a hospital, she was an insignificant patient. Mostly incomprehensible at the best of times, she was now completely so, unable to communicate and powerless. Soon, the health care system decided she and her suffering were unnecessary. When I visited her, she had no feeding tube and was given nothing orally. Helen died this way in a large Catholic hospital.

Though abandoned by the powerful, she didn't die alone. Other insignificant women—women she'd met at the Mission where she served by folding laundry—kept vigil at her bedside those last few days of her life. Perhaps they knew what it meant to be alone. Perhaps they were the kind of women who went before dawn to the tomb of an outcast man who died a criminal's death. Women who had the courage to face not only death, but also cruelty and despair.

When the women went to the tomb the first Easter morning to face death, they found something more unbearable: emptiness. Loss upon loss. Not even a body to anoint.

The final failure. And they found a vision, "two men in clothes that gleamed like lightning," and a voice that filled them with fear: "He is not here, he has risen." They were bewildered and afraid. When they obeyed the angels and told their story, they were disbelieved.

The places we tend to run away from—emptiness, fear, confusion—are the places where the Easter proclamation rings out for the first time in history. It's not the strong and powerful who were first entrusted with this word; it's the weak and insignificant. Nor was it received at first with gladness but with doubt and dismay.

It's in our emptiness that the word is most clearly given. The resurrection is best glimpsed through tears, as Mary Magdalene saw it.

Nor is it hard to find; actually, it's hard to avoid. The problem is that place of emptiness and poverty it comes out of.

That's the secret everybody now has access to: Good Friday and Easter Sunday are one day. We don't escape death or suffering, and running away from the cross doesn't help. What helps is that love meets us on our cross.

If we make Christianity a hiding place from suffering and sin, we will have trouble ever meeting Christ, for that's where he comes to find us.

Death confronted me when I visited Helen for the last time and heard her last breath. By our world, which had already cruci-

ON BECOMING BREAD

fied her, she was judged and found unworthy of life. My failure to alter that verdict has never left me.

Yet when I speak Helen's name, the word that comes with it is glory. The glory of her heart in which love triumphed daily. Of the communion with the women at her bedside. Of those who wept for her death. Of her undoubtedly joyful welcome into the Kingdom by the one who claimed his own with the words: "Today, you will be with me in Paradise."

SECTION TEN

Witness

Beauty in the mirror

Dave waved hello. His good looks were obscured by haggard gray gauntness, somewhat incongruous under the curly hair and jaunty boyish cap. He asked me how I was, flicked his cigarette, and nodded: "I'm OK. I'm back on drugs, but it's all good."

How can he ever be free of this affliction before it crushes him (and possibly those around him) completely? He was introduced to hard drugs at the age of nine by his mother. Thirty years later, it's difficult to hold out hope for his recovery, outside a miracle.

A miracle! Why not? Couldn't God heal this man? It's easy to say "God could heal anybody," and maybe easy to believe. Yet how can this person be healed of this festering wound?

If you grew up Catholic, you probably recall the strange sensation of crossed beeswax candles caressing your neck as the priest murmured a prayer for healing on the feast of St. Blaise. Blaise (Vlasios, Blasius, or Biagio), an Armenian bishop, has had a huge following since his fourth-century death. He's celebrated lovingly in Eastern and Western Christianity, though little is known of his life.

We know he was put to death for his faith in Christ and is considered a healer. Our desperate need of healing is reflected in the fervent honor paid him through the centuries. He is associated with neck and throat ailments because, first, as he was being taken to his execution, a woman brought him her son with a fishbone stuck in his throat. Through Blaise's prayers the boy was healed.

Stories of miraculous cures may seem unhelpful, especially when our own wounds chafe. Still, we need to treasure and retell these stories of healing. They remind us that healing is divine work. When we help bring healing, we become God-like.

St. Blaise heals only by the power of God, whose help he begs.

The second reason we associate him with neck and throat ailments is because Blaise died by a sword blow to the neck. It's curious that we entrust our necks to one who died from a neck wound, but healing comes in the place of greatest vulnerability.

Consider Elena, who grew up with a deep sense of shame in herself. She knew she was intelligent and could do many things but didn't believe she was really worth anything. When a relationship ended painfully, she was afflicted in her vulnerable spot: she felt unworthy of love. How cruel, when we are wounded right where we need to be healed. How astonishing, when out of that greater wounding comes greater healing.

One day Elena was trying on clothes in a shop. She looked at herself in the mirror; beside her was a pretty young girl, whose reflection Elena also could see. "Well, at least there is one beautiful thing in that mirror." Elena walked away not knowing she had spoken aloud. To her surprise, a man hurried after her. The father of the young girl, he'd heard Elena's words and came to say: "There were two beautiful women reflected in that mirror."

Elena remembers that moment as a turning point. She began to hear and accept herself as love-worthy.

Healing comes in the particular way each person needs. It comes in its own time. It can be agonizing. It has definitive moments yet is continual.

If you read for yourself the story of Blaise, you will find many other stories—the seven women taken prisoner for their devotion to him, the woman with the lost pig. The story of Blaise cannot be told on its own. That's how healing happens too.

How then can Dave's addiction be healed? Does Elena's story, or Blaise's, make any difference? They give hope, illustrating that healing is always possible. They show the value of shared suffering and never giving up on anyone. They show that escaping vulnerability is not always the best answer.

In the strange otherness of God's ways, it may be that Dave's deep vulnerability is where God most loves to dwell, and from where Dave's healing will come—at a time we don't know.

Seeing the unseeable

First Woman: "There's one at Yonge and Finch. I've heard it's good."

(Me—to myself, overhearing in the fitness center change room: "A club? A restaurant?")

First Woman: "I'm not sure if it's Lutheran or Catholic."

(Me—to myself: "I'm imagining she said that.")

Second Woman: "I've been going to church for a while. I tried St. Andrew's."

They were, accidentally but unabashedly, "witnessing" their faith. Listening to their conversation, audible throughout the change room, I pondered. Why not speak to people about my faith? Nobody in this gym, to which I'd long belonged, had any idea I'm Christian. Here were two seekers freely, and loudly, discussing their faith in a secular setting.

Being a witness is a Christian duty, and joy. If I experience something wonderful, there's an impulse to tell others. It's just too good not to share! Last week I visited friends who delighted in showing off their brand-new baby. "Who could be interested in anything else?" they seemed to say.

Pope Paul VI said people listen to teachers only if they are witnesses. Witnessing means speaking not just from the head but from the inner depths. The first people acclaimed saints were martyrs—people who witness to the point of death. The church has always had a special love for martyrs, beginning with Stephen.

Not because the church worships death; that's a contemporary cultural affliction. Rather, because "love for life didn't deter them from death," as an ancient hymn has it.

Who are the martyrs, the witnesses, in our world? The women in the gym dared to bring God into a seemingly godless place. I know people who tell their coworkers they're going out at lunchtime, not to a restaurant but to Mass. We may take risks with our career lives, or our social lives, to express our love of God. Stephen didn't live his life knowing he'd be a martyr. Nor do we know how our love of God will require our lives. This may mean standing up for life against the push for euthanasia, abortion, experimentation, or other abuses of vulnerable human life. Or against the economic imperative to promote our wealth at the expense of the poor. It may mean seeing what the world prefers to hide.

A photograph from 1993 gave witness, and perhaps cost the photographer his life (his death at thirty-three was by suicide). It features a tiny child bent over with weakness, hunger, and weariness. In the background is a waiting vulture. Photographer Kevin Carter stepped aside from the journalists covering a food station in starving Sudan and discovered this hidden, lone child—a tiny human life, completely bereft of others' care, about to become an animal's meal.

Like the Sudanese child, the Holy Innocents were little ones whose lives were extinguished by power and greed (Matthew 2:16–18). These children were born into the world at the very moment when angels were revealing God's glory and singing of peace on Earth, murdered to protect earthly power. Their killing came indirectly because of Jesus' birth—through the Magi, the wise ones who visited both the power of the King and the poverty of the Bethlehem manger.

They remind us, as does the dying Sudanese child, that even the Prince of Peace's arrival on earth doesn't produce instant peace but instant martyrdom. God doesn't impose peace upon us; he woos it out of our free will, wedded as it is to sin and violence.

Christ came for this: to overpower us with God's love, coming not to the king's palace but to a poor young couple. He came with a love that draws love out of us, beyond our capacity to sacrifice our own children to our fears—whether by the sword like Herod, or by abortion like contemporary custom, or by neglect as with the nameless Sudanese child.

There is only one gift: *caro verbum factum est*, the Word made flesh, God-with-us, just as we are. What if we, too, gave that gift to one another? What kind of witness would we give?

God comes to the betrayed

How do we cope with the pain of betrayal, especially when it comes from family?

Consider Jen, whose mother, Kristen, gave birth to her as a teenager. Kristen wanted an abortion but couldn't get one; she'd slipped into a drug addiction that would last twenty years. She kept the child and raised her, with some help from her family and occasional help from the various men in her life, mostly fellow addicts. By the time she was twelve, Jen had learned much about, shall we say, adult entertainment. She's spent much of the rest of her life trying to distance herself from her upbringing, discover a healthy sexuality, and find how to be in real relationships. Her anger against her mother is unabated; for Jen, betrayal and hurt came not from outside, but from within, from the one who should offer protection and comfort, support and nourishment. One of her biggest challenges is to learn to trust. By now, Jen knows how to cope, but she also needs to be healed.

Such stories aren't new. Many Old Testament stories about evil and sin focus on intimate betrayal, from Cain, to Joseph's eleven brothers, Delilah, and so on. In the New Testament, betrayal comes not among blood siblings but within the new family of Christ himself. The most spectacular betrayal is by Judas, but nearly all Jesus' disciples betray him by abandonment or complete denial, as with Peter. The sting Jen carries is unique to her, but it connects her with human history and its undercurrent of betrayal.

Australian Mary MacKillop (1842–1909) teaches how there can be an antidote to Jen's, and our, experience of betrayal. Some years ago, on a visit to Sydney, I had a chance encounter with Mary. One of the Sisters there gave me a tour of the motherhouse, including a museum that depicted Mary's life story and her founding of the Josephite community. Mary's courage and and the love her community bears for her are evident. So is her understanding of people in poverty and on the outskirts of society.

Four years after she established the Josephite community to accompany and serve the poor, without warning Mary was excommunicated by her bishop. Suddenly, the community's schools were closed, and forty-seven nuns were left homeless. The explanation was that Bishop Sheil disapproved of her community's ways, though other possible reasons have been put forward, including her exposing wrongdoing by clergy.

In any case, Mary felt betrayed by the church. Have you ever been in such a place, where those you trusted seemed to turn against you? Perhaps you thought you were following God's word, with faith as your guide, and suddenly you were assaulted and felled, as though you were evil. In such a place, Mary found herself echoing Psalm 22 on the lips of Jesus: "My God, my God, why have you forsaken me?"

In the museum, I read a letter written during Mary's excommunication, in which she expresses the bitter experience of betrayal, along with gratitude for those who gave her refuge. The refuge was the housing friends offered her and her sisters. Even more poignant, the local Jesuit community continued, quietly, to give her the sacraments. Though canonically outside the church, she continued to taste communion through those who held her in it despite the risk.

With such help from her community, Mary was able not only to cope with betrayal but also to pass through it to the other side of bitterness, to healing and new life. Five months afterward, as he was dying, the bishop apologized to her and lifted the excommunication.

My encounter with Mary sustains me in moments when I don't know whom to trust, including me. It reminds me that when I can't get to him, God comes to me. And that Jen's hope of healing and new life is not in vain: there's a power strong enough to heal and transform betrayal itself, bringing a new and more abundant life.

Why did God become human?

A task I enjoy is teaching theology to Catholic teachers. They are engaged in the faith, having the responsibility of evangelizing our youngest.

After one class on Christology, a teacher-student named Bill said to me, quite seriously: "Are you saying the church teaches that Jesus was actually God? God really became a human person? I don't know if I believe that!"

It's a shocking doctrine, Bill realized. How wonderful that he listened and heard it. More surprising is that it often goes unnoticed. Yes, the church teaches this: God became human!

There are plenty of good reasons *not* to become human. My friend Elinor could list dozens without stopping for breath. Elinor and her siblings grew up in spite of themselves, in an atmosphere of drunkenness and violence. As an adult, she took to city streets, getting high on every possible substance. Years later, her body has paid a high price. She's endured several operations and daily suffers physical indignities that remind all too much of one's humanness. Did God become that? Isn't it unbecoming? Why would he want what the rest of us would rather get out of?

Now on the other hand, there are delightful aspects of being human. The other day I was invited to a tea party with three little girls, who took turns whispering secrets in my ear: "psst psst psst...psssssst!" They loved the sounds, the secrecy, the feeling of whispering in somebody's ear. Meanwhile they enjoyed the color of the tea, the feel of the cups, finding out what would happen if you tipped way over on the chair, and many other dimensions of sheer humanness. Could it be that God became human for the fun of it?

Such questions hearken back to the early church's great Christological debates. People questioned (some completely rejected) the notion that in Christ, God became fully human. Exploring the question meant exploring what it means to be human. Christ leads us to the truth of our humanity.

Gospel stories suggest he enjoyed his humanity, watching wildflowers, rising bread dough, people. And he touched people in thoroughly human ways, washing dirty feet, holding children, letting them touch him.

Elinor's story reminds us God became human to share our struggles and help us "know you're with me, whatever I go through" (to quote singer Bruce Cockburn). The tea party reminds us God became human to share the delights of his own creation; "God saw what he had created, and it was good" (Genesis 1). Above all, God became human to fulfill humanity's deepest human longing: to be united with God.

One of the great leaders who arose during those early-church debates (often heated), about whether Christ is both divine and human, was Athanasius. He was a theologian and bishop of Alexandria in the fourth century—a tumultuous, pivotal time for Christianity. At an Easter Vigil long ago, I first heard the name of Athanasius in the litany of saints, and wondered about him. He helped connect Eastern and Western Christianity and made immense personal sacrifices to help be sure people understood what salvation in Christ means. Athanasius summed up tradition this way: "God became human so that humans might become divine."

In becoming human, Christ reveals what humanity is. And in showing us our humanity, he brings us face-to-face with the most profound part of our being: our desire to become God-like. There is a longing in us that can be met only by God himself.

St. Athanasius brings us back, uncompromisingly, to the church's treasury of truth. It may not be reasonable, may be disturbing, and may (let's hope) cause us to lose the ground we stand on and look at everything in a new way, as Bill did. As the two Emmaus disciples did, in the moment of breaking bread (Luke 24:13–35), when their eyes were opened and they recognized Jesus.

Epilogue

In a black boat

I sailed the silent sea

its prow piercing

the still surface where

cold path of fire

drew my vessel towards

the great full moon

almost touching

never touching

the dark edge

OF RELATED INTEREST

Benedictine Promises for Everyday People
Staying Put, Listening Well, Being Changed by God
RACHEL M. SRUBAS

In our noisy and hectic world, it can be tempting to look at the quiet, prayerful pace of life in a monastery and wish we were there. But Rachel Srubas knows that we don't need to move to a monastery to tap into the spiritual wisdom of those who do. In this engaging, spiritual, and very down-to-earth book, she shows us how the three promises of the followers of St. Benedict—staying put, listening well, and being changed by God—can be applied to our everyday lives, no matter our situation.

136 PAGES | $14.95 | 5½" X 8½" | 97816278554412

God Plays a Purple Banjo
and 41 Other Stories of Inspiration, Hope and Humor
S. JAMES MEYER

This refreshing, delightfully written, and deeply personal book provides the answer to the age-old question, "Where is God?" Everywhere, says S. James Meyer—homeless advocate, business owner, permanent deacon, husband, father, and son of a carpenter. Each of the stories here uses the stuff of everyday life to remind us that every breath we take is an encounter with God, and that there is no moment in our lives that is not sacred.

128 PAGES | $14.95 | 5½" X 8½" | 9781627854429

Scripture Passages that Changed My Life
Personal Stories from the Writers of Living Faith

Ten of *Living Faith* magazine's most well-known authors each explain how meditating on the Word of God has changed their lives. Allow the lessons that they have learned to deepen your prayer experience and maybe even change your life.

112 PAGES | $12.95 | 5½" X 8½" | 9781627853569